BEGNNINGS IN INDIA

BEGNNINGS IN INDIA

EUGENE STOCK, D.C.L.

GYAN

Published by

GYAN

Gyan Publishing House
5, Ansari Road
Daryaganj, New Delhi-110002
Phone: 011-47034999, 9811692060
E-mail: books@gyanbooks.com

Distribution Network
gyanbooks.com
India, USA, Canada, UK, Australia, France

ISBN: 978-81-212-8903-0 (PB)
First Published, 1917

2nd Impression 2023

Printed at: Gyan Press, Delhi.

BEGNNINGS IN INDIA

AUTHOR: EUGENE STOCK

BEGINNINGS IN INDIA

BY

EUGENE STOCK, D.C.L.

CENTRAL BOARD OF MISSIONS

AND

SOCIETY FOR PROMOTING CHRISTIAN KNOWLEDGE

LONDON: 68, HAYMARKET, S.W.

1917

PREFATORY NOTE

THIS book has been written at the request of the Central Board of Missions, and, as I understand, is to be one of a series of small and popular books on Missions Overseas. The subject, which was given to me, is perhaps not quite clearly indicated in the title. It is not the *Beginning* of Anglican Missions in India as one great enterprise. It is the *Beginnings* of different sections or departments of that enterprise; and some of these Beginnings were much later than the general Beginning. A glance, however, at the Table of Contents will make all clear.

My instructions were to tell of Anglican Missions, and the book is in the main confined to them. But Xavier, Carey, Duff, and other distinguished missionaries not of our communion, find incidental mention. I should gladly have told of the work of other Missions if the scope of the book, and its limited size, had permitted.

Another necessary limitation has been to India proper. Burma and Ceylon are not included, although they are both in the Ecclesiastical Province of India and Ceylon.

There is scarcely anything in these pages that has not appeared in print before, much of it in many forms. But new books on old subjects are continually needed for new generations of readers. I humbly commend this one to the Divine Blessing.

E. S.

September, 1917.

CONTENTS

BEGINNINGS IN INDIA

I

THE FIRST ANGLICAN MISSION

It was in the spacious days of great Elizabeth that England first came in touch with India. On the last day of the sixteenth century, December 31, 1600, Queen Elizabeth granted a royal charter to "one Body Corporate and Politick, in Deed and in Name, by the name of *The Governor and Company of Merchants of London trading into the East Indies.*" Thus was born the famous East India Company; and for 258 years it represented the British Power in the supremely wonderful land which became the choicest jewel in the British Crown.

India, therefore, was in one important respect unlike some other mission fields. In Nigeria, for instance, in East Africa and Uganda, on the Congo and the Zambesi, in Madagascar and New Zealand and the Southern Seas, the missionary preceded the trader and the consul and the commissioner. But in India trade led the way, so far at least as British Missions are concerned. Francis Xavier's work, indeed, was earlier than Elizabeth's reign, but not earlier than the mercantile settlements of Portugal.

Did the new Company take any steps to introduce

Christianity into India? That is not the purpose of a commercial company, as such. But what of its individual members and agents? Had they been Mohammedans, they would have carried their religion with them as a matter of course, not merely as their personal profession, but with a view to its spread among the heathen peoples. The average Moslem trader is a Moslem missionary. But it rarely occurs to the British traveller or settler or merchant that the religion he professes is for all men, that it in fact conveys messages from the Creator of the universe to the whole body of mankind, that every individual of every nation has a right to hear such messages, and that for those who have heard them to tell those who have not is an obvious duty, dictated even by common sense. The plain fact is that so many professing Christians care very little about those Divine Messages, even for themselves; why, therefore, should they trouble about other people? When Lord Macartney went to China in 1793 on an embassy from the British Government, he made this humiliating declaration: "The English never attempt to dispute the worship or tenets of others; they have no priests or chaplains with them, as have other European nations."

No special blame, therefore, attaches to the East India Company if its members simply acted as most other men act; and the fact is that both the Company and its members did more for Missions than might have been expected.

Throughout the seventeenth century, however, no steps were taken by Great Britain in any way to make known to the Indian peoples the Divine Messages to mankind. But the close of that century marked an epoch in the history of Missions. In 1698 was founded the Society for Promoting Christian Knowledge and in 1701 the Society for the Propagation of the Gospel in Foreign Parts. Now it was in the former year that Parliament, revising the East India Company's Charter, was induced by Dean Prideaux and Archbishop Tenison to add a new clause, directing that the chaplains whom the Company was sending out for its increasing number of mercantile agents "should apply themselves to learn the language of the country, the better to enable them to instruct the Gentoos (Gentiles or heathen) who should be the servants or slaves of the Company in the Protestant religion." But the Company could not be expected to do more than instruct its own "Gentoo" servants; and very many, probably the majority, of these were Portuguese or English half-castes, who came to be known as Eurasians.* So the fact remains that Great Britain, though calling itself a Christian country, had still no plan for the evangelization of India.

We must not forget, however, that there were already two large bodies of Indian Christians: (1) the ancient Syrian Church of Malabar, of which we shall hear more by-and-by; (2) the Roman Catholic descendants of the converts made by the labours of the heroic Jesuit, Francis Xavier, and his successors. The fisherman caste of South India, in particular, had been largely influenced by the Roman Missions, the centre of which was at Goa, on the west coast.

But that epoch was not without its influence on India. The foundation of the S.P.G. stirred up the

* They are now generally called Anglo-Indians, and that term can no longer be applied, as hitherto, to Englishmen in India.

zeal of Continental Protestants, and that in two directions. (1) The King of Prussia, hearing of King William III. of England having patronized the new S.P.G.—*i.e.*, by granting it a charter—arranged to add to a Philosophical Society which had just been formed at Berlin an "Oriental College" "for the propagation of the Christian faith and worship and virtue"; and some leading members of it were elected to membership of the S.P.G.* (2) The fact that the S.P.G. was to send missionaries to "the Western Indies" led to a Danish plan for sending a Mission to "the Eastern Indies," a Mission which in its turn brought the S.P.C.K. into the Indian missionary enterprise. This was the "Danish-Halle Mission," the first undertaken in India by any section of Reformed Christendom.

Denmark had two or three small trading settlements in India, and King Frederick IV., influenced partly by his chaplain, Dr. Lütkens, and partly by the news of the formation in England of a society for propagating the Gospel, was led in 1705 to reflect that "for ninety years there had been a Danish East India Company; for ninety years Danish ships had sailed to Tranquebar; Danish merchants had traded and grown rich in the settlement, Danish governors had ruled it, Danish soldiers had protected it; but no ship had ever carried a Danish missionary to preach the Gospel."† "Find me missionaries," said the King to Lütkens; and Lütkens, who was in touch with the leaders of the Pietist movement in Germany, Spener at Berlin, and Francke at Halle, applied to the latter, who sent him a young

* *Two Hundred Years*, p. 468. The fuller particulars in the S.P.G. Reports are curiously interesting.

† W. Fleming Stevenson: *Dawn of the Modern Mission*, p. 56.

Saxon, Bartholomew Ziegenbalg, and a fellow-student of his, H. Plutschau. These two young men the Danish King sent out at his own expense to the settlement at Tranquebar, a town on the Coromandel coast south of Madras, in the midst of a dense Tamil population. The story of the arrival and landing of these two pioneers, of the opposition of the Danish governor and their consequent trials, of their extraordinary industry and patience and devotion, is one of the most thrilling in the whole history of Missions. No truer missionary then Ziegenbalg ever went to heathendom. His greatest work was the translation of the New Testament and part of the Old into the Tamil language, the first Indian version of the Scriptures; an imperfect version, of course, as all first attempts must be, but which formed the basis of later revisions.

The first reports from Ziegenbalg were translated into English by A. W. Boehm, chaplain to Prince George of Denmark (the husband of our Queen Anne), and dedicated to the S.P.G., which purchased and distributed 500 copies. A box of books and a contribution of £20 were sent out to Tranquebar by the Society in behalf of some of its members, and the S.P.C.K. undertook to receive further funds for the Mission. In 1715 Ziegenbalg visited Europe, and, coming to England, was welcomed by the Archbishop of Canterbury and by King George I. Returning to India, he died in 1719, at the age of thirty-six, leaving behind him 355 Tamil converts, some schools, the Tamil Scriptures just mentioned, and a Tamil dictionary and grammar. Others went out, mostly Germans from Halle; hence the name " Danish-Halle

Mission." One of them, Schulze, was a learned scholar and a capable organizer, and under him the Mission expanded to places far beyond the small Danish territory. Madras itself was occupied in 1726.

The S.P.C.K. helped the Danish Mission from time to time, and in 1728 it formally began its own Indian work by adopting the new Madras Mission under Schulze. Two years later, it sent out, for the first time, its own missionaries, Sartorius and Geisler. These, and their successors, Fabricius, Guericke, and others, were obtained from Germany, and were in Lutheran orders.

The two Missions helped each other, and in fact worked almost as one. The length of service of several men was notable. Three or four laboured half a century. Few ever came home; they went out to live and to die. Mission centres multiplied in the Tamil country, from Madras southward to Tinnevelly. There were many difficulties, and not a few dangers. England and France were at war more than once, and French Roman Catholic missionaries had to be expelled, like the Germans of our own day. Madras was twice bombarded by French ships, and once actually occupied for a time by French troops. The Sultans of Mysore, who were allies of France, Haidar Ali and Tippu Sahib, were among the most powerful foes that we have had to fight in India.

One of the missionaries bore a name that will ever stand high in missionary records. Christian Frederic Schwartz went out in 1749, and died in 1798, and all through that half-century he was a power in the country. His Life, by Dean Pearson of Salisbury, is a chief authority for the period of his career. He originally belonged to the Danish Mission, but for the last thirty years of his life he was an East India Company's chaplain, and also associated with the S.P.C.K. He was successively at Trichinopoly and Tanjore, both famous places, the one for its lofty rock and fort, the other for its great temple of Siva, the finest in India; and both familiar S.P.G. stations in the next century and to-day. His influence was remarkable, over both Europeans and Indians. No other missionary has wielded such political authority. What in anyone else might be dangerous and compromising to a Mission became in Schwartz a power for good. The commander of the British force in South India, Colonel Fullerton, wrote in 1783: "The knowledge and integrity of this irreproachable missionary have retrieved the character of Europeans from imputations of general depravity." The Government employed him on a special embassy to Haidar Ali, who had indeed asked for him. "Send me the Christian," he said; "him I can trust"; and he received the missionary with all honour. When the British authorities insisted on supervising the kingdom of Tanjore, which had been misgoverned, Schwartz was appointed one of the three commissioners for the purpose, and for several years he may almost be said to have governed that small state. The Rajah of it, when he died, committed his young adopted son and expected successor to the missionary's care. The governor of Madras put the late Rajah's brother over the kingdom instead; but Schwartz appealed to the Governor-General at Calcutta, Lord Cornwallis, and obtained a reversal of this appointment, and he himself became Regent. Another governor-general, Lord

Teignmouth, wrote officially of him to the Company in language showing that Schwartz did not let his political position spoil his missionary work: "I have never heard his name mentioned without respect, who is as distinguished for the sanctity of his manners as for his ardent zeal in the promulgation of his religion; whose years, without impairing his understanding, have added weight to his character." When he died, the young Rajah ordered a monument to him to be put up in the garrison church at Tanjore, and this monument, which was executed by Flaxman, may be seen there to this day.

The results of these Missions were great, for a time. At least 50,000 Tamils were baptized before the close of the century. But the work did not last. Many joined the Christian Church because of the "royal priest of Tanjore," as Schwartz was called, although he never used that influence to draw them; and they were baptized too hastily. The missionaries had before them the example of the Jesuits in this respect, and not in this respect only. They followed it also in tolerating idolatrous customs, and in allowing the retention by the converts of their caste distinctions. They thought to make Caste a friend, on the mistaken ground that it was only, or mainly, a question of social status; whereas it is essentially religious, and destructive of St. Paul's principle, "All one in Christ Jesus," and therefore an unchanging enemy to Christianity. Moreover, many of them engaged in commerce or agriculture, not for selfish purposes but to spend more upon their work; and then, by helping the poorer converts with money, they created in them a sense of dependence, and gave occasion to sneers about "rice

Christians," who fell away when the doles ceased. Thousands of converts eventually relapsed to heathenism, and by the close of the century the numbers were much reduced, though spread over a wide area. The Missions also, both the Danish at Tranquebar and the more extensive S.P.C.K. work, languished for lack of men and means. In the later years of the century few Germans came forward, and Dr. Warneck, the ablest of the historians of Missions, attributes this to the withering influence of the growing rationalism. And in England there were no men for the work, and very little money. The eventual revival of the S.P.C.K. Mission did not come till the transfer of the whole work to the S.P.G. in the nineteenth century.

These Tamil Missions must be regarded as the first work of the English Church for the evangelization of the Indian peoples, although the missionaries were all German or Danish Lutherans. They were occasionally assisted by the few Company's chaplains; they used the Prayer-Book, and when necessary conducted English services; they regularly reported to the S.P.C.K., and S.P.C.K. funds were the main source of their support. It may be assumed that the Society, and Churchmen generally, however sympathetic with non-episcopal Missions, would have preferred to have for their own work English clergymen and Bishops over them; but in the absence of these they were willing to recognize Lutheran orders. When Schwartz, in 1790, ordained an excellent Tamil catechist named Satyanadan to be a "country priest" (as he was called), the S.P.C.K. recorded the fact with satisfaction. "If we wish," said its Report, "to establish the Gospel in India, we ought in time to give the natives a Church of their own independent of our support . . . and secure a regular succession of truly apostolical pastors, even if all communication with their parent Church should be annihilated." And so late as 1813, when, after many years without a single recruit, the Society had at last a German named Jacobi to send, Archdeacon Middleton delivered a charge to him—a very able and interesting address—expressing warm appreciation of the work of his predecessors and of the "country priests" ordained by Schwartz and others. And this was the Middleton who in the very next year was consecrated first Bishop of Calcutta.

II

THE FIRST WORK IN BENGAL

FROM Madras, if we went northward to Calcutta, we should to-day find there also extensive Missions of both the S.P.G. and the C.M.S., alike in the capital and in rural Bengal; also the devoted women of the Church of England Zenana Society; also the important Oxford Mission, of which more by-and-by. But if we wish to see the oldest outward and visible sign of missionary enterprise, we shall be taken to a church originally erected by the first missionary to the non-Christian population who lived and worked in Calcutta. It was built in 1771, and, though largely rebuilt long after, is still called the Old Church. From that church and its influence we may trace the beginnings of Anglican Missions in Bengal.

Calcutta was described in those old days as "a corrupt city," and the expression was used, not of the native population, but of the European community. If this were so, can we reasonably be surprised? It used to be said, in the days when ships for India sailed round the Cape of Good Hope, that men left any religion they had at the Cape, and in later times, since the direct route by the Red Sea was opened up, that the authority of the Ten Commandments ceased at Suez. These caustic sayings were not wholly unwarranted; and even now, what impression do we get from modern novels of Indian society? But there have been brilliant examples of true Christian life, nevertheless, as we shall see, not only among the chaplains, as we might expect—though Lord Teignmouth did declare that "a black coat was no security" against "the general relaxation of morals"—but also among the British officials and others, both military and civilian.

To Calcutta, in 1758, came a young Swedish Lutheran clergyman, J. L. Kiernander, from the Missions in the South noticed in our last chapter. He was kindly received by Clive, the British General who in the preceding year had won the Battle of Plassey, and thereby laid the foundation of the British Indian Empire. The welcome was all the more hearty because at the moment there were no chaplains of the Company in Bengal. The last two had perished in the Black Hole of Calcutta. It was Kiernander who built the Old Church, generously spending on it £12,000, which came to him through two marriages. It is all the more sad, after this, to find that in his later years heavy debts led to the church being seized by his creditors. Then Charles Grant, an official of the East India Company, who held the high rank of Senior Merchant, stepped forward, with the help of friends bought the church, and wrote to the S.P.C.K. for a clergyman to take charge.

The S.P.C.K. did send a Cambridge man, the Rev. A.T. Clarke, in 1789. He may be regarded as the first English clergyman to go to India as a missionary, for although the Old Church was chiefly attended by English and Eurasians, and there was little work among the non-Christian population, its then title, "the Mission Church," was justified by its unofficial position and the influence it exerted. But he only stayed a year, and then left for a chaplaincy in the south. After a few years' vain search for another Englishman, the Society sent a German Lutheran, Ringletaube; but he likewise soon went off, and joined first the Moravians and then the London Missionary Society. No wonder the S.P.C.K., referring to Schwartz, and his comrades in the South, said, "It has been the surprise of many, and the lamentation, that fortitude thus exemplified should not have inspired some of our own clergy with an emulation to follow and to imitate these champions of the Cross."*

Meanwhile, Charles Grant had evolved a scheme for a kind of "National Mission" to Bengal—national in the sense that it was to be patronized and supported by the East India Company. Of course the Company was by this time no mere commercial association. It was the governing power in the British possessions in India, so its responsibilities were far greater than they had been at first. Wilberforce, therefore, when the periodical revision of the Charter came before Parliament in 1793, moved certain clauses to give effect to the scheme. In the present day we should all understand that for the British Government to engage directly in missionary work would be a mistaken policy; but in those days, and for long after, the State was expected to share in, and practically to control, Church enterprises. The very phrase, "our happy Establishment," so common then in speeches and writings, expressed much more than our modern approval of an established Church. The defeat of Wilberforce's clauses by the East India Company

* Quoted by Dr. G. Smith, *Henry Martyn*, p. 136.

cannot be fully explained by our supposing a clearer perception on the Company's part of what is wise and right. In point of fact, many of its members would have vehemently endorsed the opinion of the great Governor-General, Warren Hastings, that "all missionary efforts should be discouraged." Much stronger language than that was used both in the Court of Directors and in Parliament.

The Company, as represented in Madras, had always shown favour to the S.P.C.K. missionaries. It had given them free passages to India. It had used them to supplement the services of the chaplains. It had even built churches for them.* How it availed itself of the great influence of Schwartz we have seen. But Madras was not Bengal, and the Calcutta Government rarely showed the liberality of the Madras authorities. The years between the defeat of Wilberforce and the next revision of the Charter in 1813 have been called the Dark Period, and if the evidence of authorities familiar with Indian history, like Marshman, Sir John Kaye, and Dr. George Smith, can be relied on, dark it certainly was, although no doubt exaggerated language has been used regarding it.

Anglican Missions in Bengal, therefore, were, as the eighteenth century closed, still in the future. But Carey the Baptist was just beginning his great work in India. He had gone out in 1793, not without difficulty, for he could not get a permit from the Company, and the captain of the ship in which he had taken his passage put him on shore again, and he then managed to get

* Interesting particulars are given in Mr. Penny's *The Church in Madras*. This book, though one-sided, does usefully correct some common misconceptions.

away in a Danish vessel. Arrived in Bengal, he had to be employed by Mr. Udny, a friend of Grant's, as manager of an indigo factory, for five years, reporting himself to the authorities annually. "If I were to return myself as a missionary," he wrote, "I should not be able to remain in the country." Meanwhile, he studied the languages and began his translations of the Scriptures. In 1799 his two famous comrades in years to come, Marshman and Ward, succeeded in getting to Calcutta in an American ship, and, on being ordered to leave India at once, contrived to escape up the river to the Danish settlement at Serampore, the governor of which refused to surrender them to the British authorities. There Carey joined them, and as the year 1800 opened, the three brethren began one of the greatest works in missionary history. Bishop Mylne of Bombay, in his valuable book on Indian Missions, compares the three famous men, Xavier, Schwartz, and Carey, and gives the palm to Carey.

There was some excuse for the hostile treatment of these and several other missionaries who were excluded from British territory—one of them Judson, the American hero of Burma. None of them belonged to the Church of England, and there was much doubt in those days about the loyalty of Dissenters; even Evangelical Churchmen were suspected. No one could be a member of the S.P.C.K. without independent testimony to his being "well affected to the Crown"; and even Charles Simeon, after thirty years at Cambridge, was black-balled. When Lord Wellesley, Governor-General, wanted a teacher of Bengali for a college he had projected at Calcutta for the better training of the young Englishmen sent out by the

Company, he actually appointed Carey, who was obviously the best man, when he found on inquiry that the despised missionary was "well affected" to the government. Then things looked better for a little while; but after the Serampore brethren had printed and circulated many Christian tracts, one unfortunate tract attacking the character of Mohammed was issued, and this led to renewed strictness on the part of the authorities. One Baptist missionary was invited by an officer at Agra to go up there as tutor to his children, but was sent back under a guard of heathen soldiers to Serampore by order of Lord Hastings, who said that "one might fire a pistol into a magazine and it might not explode, but no wise man would hazard the experiment."

All through this period, however, while no Anglican missionaries appeared, and all others were suspected, noble service for the cause of Christ and the Church was rendered by some of the Company's chaplains. Charles Grant had gone home and become a leading member (twice chairman) of the Board of Directors. Through his influence Simeon of Cambridge obtained appointments as chaplains for a number of men who had the true missionary spirit. It was a remarkable act of faith on Simeon's part, when such men were so sorely needed at home, and God honoured it with abundant recompense. David Brown took charge of the Old Church, served as its minister twenty-three years without extra pay (being also chaplain for the English church), and died at his post without once going home; and his influence and teaching were the chief instrument in a marked change that came over Calcutta society. Many officers and civilians became truly religious men, and the results of this change were seen for half a century and more in the fearless Christian profession of so many leading officials. Claudius Buchanan was also a real power in Calcutta, and Lord Wellesley put him at the head of the college before mentioned. Henry Martyn, the Senior Wrangler in 1801, had coveted missionary work among non-Christians, and though he eventually went out as a chaplain, he studied the languages, preached to the heathen, did valuable translational work, and died in Armenia on his way home, leaving a reputation for personal devotion to the Lord which led Sir James Stephen, in the *Edinburgh Review*, to declare that his brief career had given the Church of England its one "heroic name" (but there have been many added since then!). Daniel Corrie, afterwards first Bishop of Madras, started the first Indian evangelist of the English Church (as we shall see) when there was not a single English missionary in all India. Thomas Thomason succeeded Brown at the Old Church, and he and Corrie made it an active centre of missionary zeal and interest; and his son became in after years one of the best Governors an Indian province ever had. Marmaduke Thompson at Madras was also a power for good; so a little later were Robinson, Kerr, Hough of Tinnevelly, Fisher of Meerut, Carr of Bombay (where he was afterwards first Bishop). Some of these, and others, both from Cambridge and from Oxford, were Fellows of their colleges. In the chaplaincies, therefore, the Church may truly be said to have been represented by picked men.

But the day was now approaching when India was really to be thrown open for missionary enterprise.

Not, however, without a long struggle in England. In 1806 some Sepoy troops mutinied at Vellore, near Madras, and this was instantly attributed, though without a shadow of reason, to their alarm at the presence of the half-dozen innocent missionaries in the Madras Presidency. This not only strengthened the hostile party in India, but led to a war of pamphlets in England. Sydney Smith's famous and furious attack on Missions appeared in the *Edinburgh Review.* With glorious inconsistency, while the "consecrated cobblers" were sneered at as incompetent, their instant expulsion was demanded as the only way to save India for the British Crown. Proposals to this effect at the Court of Directors were only defeated by the strenuous efforts of Charles Grant. Even Bishop Horsley, probably the ablest of the Bishops of his day, actually said in the House of Lords, "There is no obligation upon us as Christians to attempt the conversion of the natives of India, even were it possible to do so, which I deny. The command of our Saviour to His apostles does not apply to us"!

But Wilberforce planned a new campaign as the year for a fresh revision of the Company's charter drew near. The venerable S.P.C.K. and the youthful C.M.S. set all their influence in motion, and in 1813 the decisive battle ensued. Once more the House of Commons was treated to a glowing description of Hinduism and its "benignant and softening influences," and to expressions of "horror at the idea of sending out Baptists and Anabaptists to convert such a people, disturbing institutions ordained by Providence to make them virtuous and happy." But this time Wilberforce triumphed. What, however, was the actual decision?

No official Government Mission was now proposed, as in 1793. Two resolutions were moved and carried. One acknowledged our duty "to promote the interests and happiness of the Indian peoples," and that, with a view to the introduction of "useful knowledge and religious and moral improvement," "sufficient facilities should be afforded by law to persons desirous of going to and remaining in India" to accomplish "those benevolent designs." In other words, the State left the Church, by the instrumentality of the Societies which were its arms, free to do the work for which the State was unfitted.

The other resolution, which provided for the establishment of a Bishopric, will come before us in the next chapter. Meanwhile, this chapter has shown us how truly the Old Church in Calcutta stands to this day as the representative of the earliest Anglican missionary enterprise in Bengal.

III

THE FIRST BISHOPS

In our last chapter we visited an old church in Calcutta, and its history took us back to the beginnings of missionary work in Bengal. Let us now visit another sacred building in the same city—the cathedral. On inquiry we find that it was built by the fifth Bishop of Calcutta, Daniel Wilson, who gave £20,000 out of his own pocket towards its cost and endowment; and we see on his memorial tablet the inscription directed in his will, the publican's prayer: Ὁ Θεός, ἱλάσθητί μοι τῷ ἁμαρτωλῷ, literally, "God, be propitiated to me the sinner."

It may be that we are invited to look in at a certain ecclesiastical meeting being held hard by. We enter, and find thirteen Bishops sitting—the Episcopal Council of the Province of India and Ceylon; and, in the chair, the Metropolitan, the eleventh Bishop of Calcutta. That is a clear evidence of an advanced state of Church life, a great contrast to the position, little more than a century ago, depicted in our last chapter. How and when came the first Bishop? and who was he? and what of his successors?

We have seen how in the days of George III. it was the way of many English people to expect the State to direct the work of the Church. Yet they had small encouragement for such an expectation. For 200 years England was extending its possessions and its commerce abroad, and providing a few, a very few, clergy to minister to its sailors and soldiers and consuls and merchants; and all that time there was not a single Bishop to guide and govern their work. Was that the Church's fault? Archbishop Laud began moving in 1634, and obtained from Charles I. an Order in Council extending the jurisdiction of the Bishop of London to all clergy and congregations abroad; but his efforts, and those of later Archbishops, failed to get a Bishop consecrated, even for the growing American Colonies. The S.P.G., from the very year of its foundation, appealed again and again to the Government, but in vain. Bishop Sherlock, in 1751, remarked that "for a Bishop to live at one end of the world and his Church at another must make the office very uncomfortable to the Bishop and useless to the people."* It involved, for one thing, that every candidate for holy orders in the American Colonies had to take what was then a dangerous voyage to England to be ordained, and of those who sailed one in five perished at sea.

Not till 1784 did the Church in the United States (as the Colonies had then become) obtain its first Bishop from the Scottish Episcopal Church. It was in the same year that John Wesley, despairing of the English Church ever sending Bishops to America, took the bold step of "setting apart by the imposition of hands Thomas Coke to superintend the flock of Christ"; which step in its issues led to the formation of the Methodist Episcopal Church, now so vigorous

* *Two Hundred Years of S.P.G.*, p. 743. The accounts there given of the appeals and their failure are quite pathetic. See also *Hist. C.M.S.*, Vol. i., p. 404.

and influential in America. That Church has now the largest missionary organization in India, a significant fact, suggesting the loss sustained by the Anglican Communion through the too complete subjection of the English Church to the State in those old days.

At last, in 1787, the English Church got leave from the State to send its first two Colonial Bishops to Canada. India had yet to wait twenty-seven years more. Then the agitation before referred to, which led to the opening of India to missionaries, was also directed to the foundation of the See of Calcutta. Claudius Buchanan was commissioned by the still young and unrecognized C.M.S. to write pamphlets for both objects, and these were circulated all over the country. The clause providing for the appointment of a Bishop and three archdeacons was not seriously opposed in Parliament, though the usual objection was raised that the time was "not opportune" (when is the time ever opportune for a good reform?); and the Bill received the royal assent on July 21, 1813.

The new diocese was to comprise all India and Ceylon, and—Australia! The clergyman chosen for this impossible sphere was Archdeacon Middleton, Vicar of St. Pancras, the very man who had just given so warm a send-off to Jacobi, the S.P.C.K.'s latest recruit from Lutheran Germany, as before mentioned (p. 10); a man, therefore, already interested in Missions in India. He was consecrated on May 8, 1814, in Lambeth Palace Chapel. At a farewell meeting at the S.P.C.K. house, Bishop Law of Chester expressed a hope that the new Episcopate would "stop the wild progress of enthusiasm and spread uncorrupted Christianity." "Enthusiasm" in those days was a recognized phrase for evangelical fervour, and Bishop Law's words were directed against "enthusiasts" of the type of Carey and Henry Martyn. The East India Company seems to have thought that caution was necessary in letting India know of the coming Bishop. It is said that secrecy was kept regarding his voyage and landing, for fear the Hindus should be alarmed or offended at the advent of a great chief priest of Christianity. But Sir John Kaye quaintly says:

"There was no commotion, no excitement. Offended Hinduism did not rise up in arms, nor indignant Mohammedanism raise a war cry of death to the infidel. The Bishop preached in the Christian temple, and that night the Europeans slept soundly in their beds. There was not a massacre; there was not a rebellion. It really seemed probable, after all, that British dominion in the East would survive the blow."*

Bishop Middleton was an excellent prelate for the English community in India, and bravely tackled awkward questions of jurisdiction and the like. But he was sorely perplexed what to do with missionaries to the non-Christian population. He regarded them as quite outside the range of his authorized functions, and, says his biographer, "was uniformly anxious to keep the duties of the chaplains and of the missionaries separate from each other." It was not a burning question when there were so few men concerned. The S.P.C.K. men, being Lutherans, could of course not be licensed. The S.P.G. had only one clergyman in Middleton's life-time, and it had not yet taken over the S.P.C.K. Missions The C.M.S. sent out eleven

* *Christianity in India,* p. 290.

English clergymen during his episcopate, besides Lutherans, so it was with them that the Bishop's difficulties were chiefly concerned, and his attitude, conscientious as it was, caused the Society much disappointment. Moreover, he could not see his way to ordain Indians, though the C.M.S. had much hoped that Abdul Masih (to be mentioned hereafter) would have been admitted to the ministry. In time, however, he came round, and a happy arrangement was nearly settled when he died, after an eight years' episcopate, worn out with his incessant "labour and travail"—in his case *travel*, though he never attempted Australia! But his great project was Bishop's College—of which more hereafter—in aid of which a royal letter, then an occasional custom, commanded collections in all the churches in England, which produced £45,000; and the three Societies, S.P.C.K., S.P.G., and C.M.S., each gave £5,000, the Bible Society adding a fourth £5,000 for Scripture translations. But, as we shall see, the scheme was premature, and the fine buildings and plans never fulfilled the Bishop's noble anticipations

Then came Bishop Heber, a devoted parish priest, a brilliant scholar, a true poet, a fascinating personality. "No man," wrote young Lord Ashley (afterwards the great Earl of Shaftesbury), "ever equalled Bishop Heber. His talents were of the most exquisite character. If he were not a Socrates, able to knock down by force of reasoning the most stubborn opposers, he was like Orpheus, who led even stones and trees by the enchantment of his music."* We know him best now as a hymn-writer; and truly, the author of "Holy,

* *Life of Lord Shaftesbury*, Vol. i., p. 102.

holy, holy," and "The Son of God goes forth to war," and "From Greenland's icy mountains," can never be forgotten. But his Indian journals were for half a century regarded as the most vivid description of the country ever penned. His policy was quite different from Middleton's. The man who had heard the "call" from "India's coral strand" for deliverance from "error's chain" was not likely to hesitate in giving his whole-hearted support to the missionary enterprise. He expressed "entire approval" of the principles on which the C.M.S. Missions were conducted. He arranged at once to give licences to the missionaries, and this enabled them to render occasional help to the chaplains in ministering to the English community, which they were glad to do. And he ordained two native clergymen: the first a Tamil from Ceylon, who was a student at Bishop's College; the second, Abdul Masih (see p. 46).

On April 2, 1826, Bishop Heber was at Trichinopoly, Schwartz's old station in the South, and in the Fort Church "spoke with great affection on the glorious dispensation of God in Christ Jesus, and the necessity resting on us to propagate the faith throughout India." The same day he was found dead in his bath. Universal was the grief in India; high officials addressed meetings held in memory of him at Calcutta, Madras, and Bombay. It took five months for the news to reach England, and here also the grief was extreme.

Two more episcopal lives were sacrificed in the hopeless task of superintending the whole work of the Church in India. Bishop James lived eight months, and died; Bishop Turner lived eighteen months, and died. The death of the fourth Bishop in nine years caused the utmost consternation in England. The three Societies at once memorialized the Government, urging the establishment of more Bishoprics, but political strife prevented anything being done. It was the epoch of the Reform Bill.

But who would take up the mantle of prophetical service and sacrifice dropped by the four Bishops in succession? Charles Grant, son of the former East India Director, had now the charge of India in the new Reform Ministry; and he applied to several leading clergymen without success. At last Daniel Wilson, Vicar of Islington, volunteered "to sacrifice himself if God should accept the offering." He was consecrated on April 29, 1832, went out to his great sphere, and lived and worked twenty-six years with only one visit home. One incident of his episcopate is worth noticing in passing. The first steam-vessel from England reached India in the year of Heber's death, but of course by the Cape route, and she took five months to do it, like the old sailing "East Indiamen." It was Bishop Wilson's energy and influence that inspired new schemes, and in 1841 the P. and O. Company organized the Malta, Alexandria, Red Sea route with "big" liners of 1,600 tons!

And at last came the division of the impossible diocese. Charles Grant the younger, who had become Lord Glenelg, revising the Company's charter again in 1833, made provision for the two new dioceses of Madras and Bombay (the former including Ceylon); and after two or three years' further delay, two admirable Archdeacons of long experience in India, and full of missionary zeal, were appointed—Daniel Corrie, the friend of Henry Martyn, to Madras, and Thomas

Carr to Bombay. Australia also received its own Bishop at the same time.

This is not the place to tell the whole story of the growth of the Indian episcopate. Let us only put on record the names of the Bishops. At Calcutta since Wilson, we recall Cotton, Milman, Johnson, Welldon, Copleston, Lefroy. At Madras, after Corrie, Spencer, Dealtry, Gell, Whitehead. At Bombay, after Carr, Harding, Douglas, Mylne, Macarthur, Pym, Palmer. At Lahore, French, Matthew, Lefroy, Durrant. In Travancore, Speechly, Hodges, Gill. In Chota Nagpur, Whitley, Westcott. At Lucknow, Clifford, Westcott. In Tinnevelly, Morley, Williams, Waller. At Nagpur, Chatterton. In Assam, Pakenham Walsh. Seventeen sent out from England; six East India chaplains; fourteen missionaries; two translated from other dioceses. If we add the nine in Burma and Ceylon, we have, for the Ecclesiastical Province of India and Ceylon, an apparent total of forty-eight Bishops; really forty-six, as the names of R. S. Copleston and Lefroy would be reckoned twice.

IV

THE FIRST CHRISTIAN VILLAGES

SUPPOSE we are at Allahabad, the capital of the "United Provinces of Agra and Oudh": we shall probably, besides being shown much that is interesting in the city, be invited to visit a neighbouring village embosomed in a grove of fine mango-trees, with its pleasant little church in the midst. This, we shall be told, is the Christian village of Muirabad, named after its great patron, a former Governor of the Province, Sir William Muir, and inhabited by Indian Christians employed in the city, who maintain their own church and pastor. Suppose, again, we are at Nasik, in the Deccan: here, too, we shall be invited to go two miles out of the city to the village of Sharanpur, where we find a band of Christians engaged in agricultural industries; and we shall be told how another excellent statesman, Sir Bartle Frere, Governor of Bombay, sent to this settlement the East African lads rescued in his days from the Arab slave-ships, and how Livingstone came here and got the famous "Nasik boys" who were with him in his last journeys and brought his body to England. Suppose, once more, we are at Delhi: here we find poor Christians gathered in *bastis*, small groups of houses with an open courtyard, where they can live apart from their heathen neighbours.

How came this system of segregation to be adopted?

In the early days of our Missions, the perplexing question was, what is to become of the newly baptized Indian? His trade or calling had probably a caste of its own, and no one would employ him or do business with him. Hence the commencement at many Mission Stations of industrial work, to enable converts to earn their living. In the rural districts, those with ever so little land could go on cultivating it; but often their cows would be stolen and their wells stopped. The Rev. J. L. Kearns, of the S.P.G., wrote in 1858: "The whole community combine to give the Christian no fire or water, or even to sell him food. If he is a creditor, his debtors are forbidden to pay him. Charges are got up against him, false witnesses suborned, and he is arrested and punished"—and so on.

The ideal, no doubt, would be for the Christians to live among their heathen neighbours, and seek occasions of influencing them; but this was often impracticable, so Christian settlements became common. It is in the south that they have been most useful; and we will pay them a visit in the southernmost province of British India.

The province of Tinnevelly is about the size of Yorkshire, and has been the scene of one of the most interesting of Anglican Missions, carried on by both the S.P.G. and the C.M.S. Corresponding nearly to the position of Leeds in our great county is Tinnevelly Town, dominated, as the visitor cannot help feeling, by the great temple of Siva, with its extensive grounds, numerous shrines, large revenues, and army of Brahman priests. Three miles off is another town, Palamcotta, the seat of British administration and the centre of the C.M.S. Mission. Corresponding nearly to Bridlington on the Yorkshire coast is the port of Tuticorin, an important S.P.G. station. The river Tambraparni fairly corresponds with the Humber and its affluents. On the west, as Yorkshire is bounded by the Pennine range, so is Tinnevelly by the Ghats. But the southern part of the Province, where the largest Missions are, is very different from South Yorkshire, being a vast sandy plain covered with groves of the palmyra-tree, which is in various ways the main sustenance of the people. Its sap is their food, its leaves their writing-paper, its fibres their string, its roots their drums, its trunk their timber.

The famous missionary Schwartz, of whom we read in our first chapter, twice visited Tinnevelly, and baptized a Brahman woman who had been taught by an English officer with whom she lived, and had built a little church. At Schwartz's second visit, in 1786, there was a congregation of 160 persons, and it was to minister to them that he ordained the Tamil catechist Satyanadan, before mentioned. The numbers grew to a few thousand, but when James Hough, the missionary-hearted chaplain, went to Palamcotta in 1816, he found the remnants (about 3,000) scattered among many villages, and ministered to by the Tamil "country priests." The S.P.C.K. was unable to respond to his appeal for a missionary, and in 1820 he obtained from the C.M.S. two Lutherans lately arrived at Madras, one of them, Rhenius, a man of great ability and devotion, who for nearly ten years watched over the scattered Christians. At last, in 1836, the S.P.G., which had taken over the Missions, was able to spare an English clergyman, and in 1841 came R. Caldwell, who had gone to India under the L.M.S., but joined the Church and the S.P.G. He was a great man in every way. Dr. George Smith reckons him and Duff and John Wilson as "the three most remarkable benefactors of the peoples of India."* Meanwhile, the C.M.S. Lutherans, who had yielded to anti-Church influences, had been superseded by English clergymen, among whom was Edward Sargent. Thirty-five years later, Caldwell and Sargent became Assistant Bishops together under the Bishop of Madras.

From early days the Tinnevelly Christians gathered into villages of their own. One of the earliest was Mudalur, in the S.P.G. district, where in 1841 Bishop Spencer found 1,000 people, palmyra-climbers, and declared that he "could not describe the effect on the mind" of a visit to such a "little Christian colony." From there he went to another, which the people had christened Nazareth, a name now very familiar in S.P.G. circles, and there he confirmed 441 candidates. It was at Nazareth that Caldwell preached his first sermon in Tinnevelly; and no wonder that his text was "The night is far spent, the day is at hand." It has, indeed, always been a model Mission Station, particularly under A.F. Caemmerer in early days and A. Margöschis in later times, the latter's thirty years' fruitful service ending with his death so recently as 1908. With its primary and middle and high schools, its art industrial school, its orphanage, its medical work, its success in self-support, its evangelistic preaching by the Christians themselves, we can understand how Bishop Gell of Madras could say in 1892: "In the whole Presidency there is not another place where

* *Twelve Pioneer Missionaries*, p. 186. This book, like all Dr. Smith's, is a brilliant work.

so much useful work of different kinds is going on as at Nazareth." Another early village was Sawyer-puram, named after a trader who helped the Mission in business matters, and who himself bought the land that some persecuted converts might settle on it, 500 of whom were found in 1842, without any missionary having yet come to them, besides inquirers and adherents in seventy neighbouring villages.

In the C.M.S. districts, which are more extensive, a Dharma Sangam, or Native Philanthropic Society, was formed in the time of Rhenius for the purchase of land for such villages, and several sprang up under its auspices, as Kadachapuram (Grace Village), Suviseshapuram (Gospel Village), Nallur (Good Town). One illustration may be given of the persecution endured by the poor Christians. They had transformed their little devil-temple or shrine into a chapel or "prayer-house," and the transformed hut had been pulled down in the night. In this case an appeal was made to the magistrate at Palamcotta. The members of the "Sacred Ashes Society," who had destroyed the prayer-house, pleaded that no such building had existed. The magistrate dispatched a police-officer to see the place and report. The heathen party instantly sent men to run all night and reach the village first, thirty miles off. When the policeman arrived, he was shown a bit of ploughed land, with grain growing. A Christian bystander, however, quietly said, "Please, sir, take up one or two of those blades of grain by the roots." The ground had been ploughed, watered, and planted in the night, to remove all traces of the ruined building!

One village is notable in several ways. A Welshman,

John Thomas, who landed in India on Christmas Day, 1836, and preached his first Tamil sermon on the next Christmas Day, was stationed where there was a small Christian settlement in the midst of a desert swept by storms of sand and dust. The natives called the district *sabanilam*, "soil under a curse." But Thomas resolved that the settlement should live up to its name, Mengnanapuram, "True Wisdom Village." He dug wells and created an oasis, and very soon, both physically and spiritually, the desert rejoiced and blossomed as the rose. Ten years later he crowned his work by building a large church, with a tower and tall spire, and room for 2,000 people to sit on the floor; and, as a true Welshman, he named it St. David's. Bishop Cotton wrote in 1864:

"On the floor are seated 1,400 dusky Tamils, the catechists, and schoolmasters, in full suits of white, the poorer men only with waist-cloths, the women in gay colours; the school-children massed in two squares; all profoundly attentive, kneeling reverentially in the prayers, joining heartily in the responses, listening eagerly to the sermon. It is in catechetical form: Can you finish that text? What was my second head? And an answer is given in full chorus. The more intelligent make notes on strips of palmyra leaf. The singing is soft, melodious, reverential."

Thomas continued in charge thirty-three years, and when he died, in 1870, he left 11,000 Christians in 125 villages—that is, in the Mengnanapuram "circle" alone (one of ten circles). His widow continued at the village thirty years more, and his daughter superintends an important boarding-school there to this day, after fifty years' service. The pastoral and evangelistic work has long been entirely in Indian hands, there being nine Tamil clergymen in the circle.

The whole number of Christians in Tinnevelly now exceeds 100,000, with about 100 Indian clergymen; and the church funds, for pastoral expenses, stipends of clergy and teachers under the Church Council, etc., exceed £10,000 a year. The Church has supplied doctors, lawyers, magistrates, etc., to the civil community, several of them graduates of Madras University. Although the work under the two Societies respectively is still separately administered, this is only pending the complete synodical organization of the Church under the Bishop; and meanwhile the two sections are united in spirit, and have common meetings and services from time to time. When the C.M.S. Centenary was celebrated, a Memorial Hall was erected at Palamcotta, to the cost of which S.P.G. Christians contributed as well as their brethren. When Prince Edward of Wales (afterwards Edward VII.) visited South India in 1874, he met 7,000 of the Christians gathered at a railway station, and Caldwell (not then Bishop) presented him with an address from the whole body; and the Prince replied, "It is a great satisfaction to me to find my countrymen engaged in offering to our Indian fellow-subjects those truths which form the foundation of our own social and political system, and which we ourselves esteem as our most valued possession."

Bishop Cotton, in 1864, wrote to his successor as Headmaster of Marlborough, Dr. Bradley, that he was "deeply impressed with the reality and thorough-going character of the whole business," and begged him "never to believe insinuations against missionary work in India," or "to scruple to plead in the school chapel for either S.P.G. or C.M.S." "My own faith in the Gospel," he said, "has been strengthened by the sight of what Christianity can do. 'I have heard of thee by the hearing of the ear, but now mine eye seeth thee.'"

There is a recent interesting development of the village system in the Punjab. By splendid works of irrigation the Government has reclaimed large regions between the great rivers, and these are now colonized by villagers from over-populated districts. Some thousands of these immigrants are Christians, the fruit of the recent mass movement; and, owing to the intervention of Colonel Montgomery (brother of the Bishop), certain villages have been assigned to them. One is named Montgomerywala after him, and another Batemanabad after the late distinguished missionary Rowland Bateman. The Christians are permanent tenants under Government, a status which avoids the difficulties occasioned by direct missionary ownership.

The old village system assuredly justified itself in Tinnevelly; and the new system will doubtless justify itself in the Punjab.

V

THE FIRST EDUCATIONAL MISSIONS

As we walk through the streets of an Indian town, or from village to village in the "mofussil" or rural districts, we are struck, just as we are in England, with the multitudes of children. Do they go to school? Well, King George, when he visited India, announced fresh and enlarged measures to educate them; and with good reason, for notwithstanding all that has been done in the past, only 106 per thousand of the male population at the last census could read, and only ten per thousand of the females.

Still, we do find a great many schools at work, and we find that our Missionary Societies have been in the front in providing them. It is delightful to see the scholars: little ones with brown faces, black hair, bright eyes, as full of playful life as any we have seen at home, and elder boys and girls with eyes as bright, and with a keenness in their countenances that tells of their opening and receptive minds. Let us inquire how our Church Missions came to have these schools, and when and how they began.

From the first it was felt that while adult converts were to be looked for and prayed for, their number might not be large. In the south, it was true, whole families, and even whole villages, put themselves under Christian instruction, as we have seen. But in the north there were no such movements. The converts were, like the restored Israel in Isaiah's prophecy (xxvii. 12), "gathered one by one," and the hope of any large harvest rested on the winning of the young. To bring boys and girls into schools in which the Bible was read and the Gospel taught was felt to be the surest way of sowing the seed. And while no method of evangelization has failed to give good results, it is certain that education, in one form or another, has done the best.

It was with curious caution that some of the first Mission schools were opened in Bengal. There were of course no Christian teachers who could be employed; and at the present day we read with surprise that the appointment of non-Christians was thought to be not only unavoidable but actually wise. On the very first school opened by the C.M.S. Calcutta Committee, at Kidderpore, a suburb of the capital, the Report of 1817 says: "It is under the care of the missionaries, but is not likely to alarm prejudice, as the master is not a Christian." In two or three cases officers who cared for the people opened schools. The C.M.S. Mission at Burdwan, seventy miles from Calcutta, of which John Perowne (father of three distinguished Cambridge men) and J. J. Weitbrecht (father of Dr. Weitbrecht-Stanton) were afterwards heads, began in this way. Captain Stewart, who was stationed there, opened village schools round about. There was at first no Christian teaching, and the Calcutta Committee, who supplied the money, thought this "very wise." Presently a higher school was opened in the town itself, at which English and the Bible were taught, and to which the more promising boys from the village schools were drafted. Thus, to use language which in after times described similar arrangements everywhere, the Vernacular Schools fed the Anglo-Vernacular School. After the central school had been at work for a year, the British community in the town were invited to a public examination, at which, to their astonishment, they heard Brahman boys, in the presence of their parents, reading the Gospels and answering questions on them. Another year passed, and the Scriptures (vernacular, of course) were taught in all the schools; and the Report said: "Who could have expected a year ago to see a thousand Hindu and Mohammedan boys reading the Gospels?" This is just one specimen.

Other schools, opened by officers or chaplains, but financed by the C.M.S., came gradually into work at distant North Indian cities, including Delhi. The S.P.G. Missions were confined to Calcutta and Lower Bengal until Cawnpore was occupied in 1833. But in the South, when (1826) the S.P.G. took over the old S.P.C.K. Missions, it had many schools to carry on, and Bishop Heber, in that year, declared that those at Madras were the best he had seen in India. In Bombay, also, both Societies were opening schools; here, too, with much help from an officer in the army, Captain George Candy, who was afterwards ordained, and as a chaplain rendered important service to both Missions.

Naturally, boys' schools were more numerous and more prosperous than girls' schools. Indian parents did appreciate the former; but what did girls want with education? Mrs. Marshman, however, the wife of Carey's chief colleague, was successful with her schools, and in 1820 there arrived at Calcutta a lady who made an important beginning under the C.M.S. This was Miss M. A. Cooke, whose name was quaintly entered as "an European female." She was learning Bengali, and to improve her pronunciation she, on Jan. 25, 1822, visited a boys' school. The native master was just driving away a little girl who had been pestering him for three months to let her learn with the boys. Miss Cooke said, "Let me teach her," and next day she found fifteen girls eager to be taught, while their mothers stood outside and peered through the lattice. To these mothers a friend with Miss Cooke explained that she had left country and home for the sole purpose of educating Indian girls, and with one voice they cried out, beating their breasts, "Oh, what a pearl of a woman!" Before a year was out Miss Cooke had fifteen schools at work, with Eurasian teachers, and 400 girls in attendance. A Ladies' Association for their support was formed in Calcutta, the Marchioness of Hastings, wife of the Governor-General, contributing handsomely.

Another branch of educational and philanthropic work arose out of the great famine of 1837-1838. It threw orphans by hundreds on the care of the missionaries, and orphanages became a recognized branch of missionary labour. Both the Church Societies started them, the largest being at Sikandra, near Agra, where the Government gave for the purpose a building which had been the tomb of the traditionally Christian wife of the Mogul Emperor Akbar. This and similar institutions were long superintended by Germans, not from Berlin or Halle, like the S.P.C.K. men of old, but mostly from the Basle Missionary Seminary, and in English orders. Such work was exactly suited to the special talents of these plodding missionaries. They loved to have the entire care of their people, young or old: they were the *mā-bāp* (mother and father) of all entrusted to them. Moreover, they were excellent for the industrial training commonly given. But it is probable that the large recruiting of the North Indian congregations from these orphanages has not tended to strengthen the self-reliance and vigorous life of the Church. Actual converts from Hinduism or Islam have usually more backbone than those who have been nursed from infancy. But until later years these converts were generally a small minority.

We must now turn our attention to another and much higher type of missionary education. In a tour round India we should visit many Christian High Schools and Colleges, to which the boys and youths of the upper classes are attracted by the excellence of the secular teaching. Sometimes objections to this system find utterance: "Why waste your time," it is asked, "in teaching mathematics and English literature? why not go into the streets and preach the Gospel?" Well, we do both, but in point of fact, it is from missionary High Schools and Colleges that most of the converts have come who have proved the leaders of the Indian Church. Not always are they won while pupils; more often afterwards, when some preacher or teacher may appeal to the Christian knowledge they have acquired, and so touch hearts and consciences.

This is a system which, though vigorously worked by the Anglican Missions, did not begin in them. Carey at Serampore had thought of it, as he thought of almost every good plan first, and had tried the experiment. But it owes its initiation and reputation mainly to the fine work of the Scottish Presbyterians, who have sent forth a succession of their best men to throw their strength into it. The very first missionary commissioned by the General Assembly went to India for the purpose in 1830, a brilliant young student of St. Andrews' University—Alexander Duff.

Duff's plans were not viewed favourably by the missionaries at Calcutta. "You will deluge the city," they said, "with rogues and villains." But the fact was that the dreaded deluge of "rogues and villains" revelling in Western philosophy and science had already begun. A Hindu College had been opened under the joint auspices of Englishmen and influential Hindus, strictly non-Christian, and virtually anti-Christian. The English textbooks were Hume's Essays and the licentious plays of the Stuart period. The result was a flood of immorality which alarmed respectable Hindu parents, and the whole cause of English study was discredited. Moreover, the street-preaching and vernacular schools already in vogue were effecting very little, and not touching the upper classes at all. Duff said to the objecting missionaries: "While you are separating precious atoms from the mass, we shall prepare a mine which shall one day explode and by God's blessing tear up the whole." Hinduism is not yet "torn up," though it is profoundly modified; but God gave Duff some "precious atoms," sooner than he or anyone else thought possible.

Duff had one distinguished supporter, the founder of the Brahmo Samaj, Ram Mohun Roy, who lent him a room in which to begin the school, and himself persuaded Brahman parents to send their boys. Its success as an educational institution was immediate. By the end of the first year, 300 lads were in regular attendance. Then Duff began a course of teaching on religion in his own house, and not only the more thoughtful of his own pupils, but some from the Hindu College also, eagerly drank in his words. Before the third year had run its course, four Brahman youths had been baptized. One was Krishna Mohun Banerjea, who joined the English Church, and afterwards became the leading Indian clergyman in Bengal. After five years Duff came home, and roused Scotland to send forth more of her ablest sons for similar service.* Then he went back and laboured thirty years more. Forty-eight converts from the higher castes were the crown of his efforts and prayers, and of these the large majority became preachers or teachers of the Gospel. He was followed by Wilson at Bombay and Anderson at Madras, with their great colleges on the same system. His and their influence extended all over India, and not least to the Missions of the English Church.

The first school established on Duff's principles by an Anglican Mission was in a part of India which we have not yet visited. Northward from Madras for 500 miles stretches what in missionary publications is called the Telugu country; but Telugu is not a geographical but a linguistic word. The Telugu language stands third in India in respect of the numbers speaking it, being only surpassed by Hindi and Bengali. The two Church Societies began work among these

* Duff's speeches on the subject have never been surpassed, if equalled. His address to the General Assembly occupies twenty-four columns of the *Missionary Register* of 1835.

people about the same time, 1842, the S.P.G. having a large field in the central districts, and the C.M.S. field lying further north. In 1840 an appeal for these people fell, simultaneously but independently, into the hands of an Oxford man, H. W. Fox, and a Cambridge man, Robert Noble, and they went out together in 1841. Their respective spheres of work illustrate the variety of missionary effort. Fox started itineration among the villages; Noble started a High School like Duff's. To-day the Mission has extended far and wide. The village preaching and teaching has produced a present Christian population of nearly 40,000 in the northern district alone. The teaching and influence of the school have given the Church there the majority of its leaders, clerical and lay.

Robert Noble continued in India twenty-four years without returning home, and died at his post. His school is now the Noble College, a "first-grade college" in government reckoning. It was at first a strictly caste school, admitting no pupils from the population that has supplied the bulk of the Telugu Church. To admit them would have been to exclude the Brahman and other high-caste students. But the gradual influence of the school was manifested at Noble's funeral in 1865, when his body was borne to the grave by six Christians, one a Brahman, one a Vellama, one a lower Sudra, one an out-caste Mala, one a Moslem —and an Englishman. Several of the students have been ordained, and some have filled important positions in the Church; others have been magistrates, head masters, etc. On the College staff itself there were, two or three years ago, four Brahman converts and five sons of Brahman converts.

The Noble College is one of the four first-grade colleges now worked by the C.M.S. in India, the others being at Calcutta, Agra, and Peshawar. It has also four "second-grade," and forty High Schools. St. John's College at Agra was the first, founded in 1852 by T.V. French and E. C. Stuart (afterwards Bishops of Lahore and Waiapu, N.Z.), and it is now one of the finest in India, having been in recent years particularly successful in enlisting the personal services of Oxford and Cambridge men, who have gone out on the Short Service system. The S.P.G. has first-grade colleges at Delhi and Cawnpore (which we shall visit in a future chapter), and at Trichinopoly, and second-grade colleges at Nandyal and in Chota Nagpur.

All these colleges may be regarded as indirectly fruits of Duff's work and example. Indeed, the High Schools of lower rank, reckoned as "Middle Schools," which are very numerous, may also be almost so regarded. The first and second grade colleges are all affiliated to the Indian Universities, which were first established in 1857.

Most of the colleges are primarily evangelistic in purpose; that is, they are designed to bring young non-Christians under Christian teaching and influence. But it is usual to have hostels attached to them in which the Christian boys, who naturally are increasing in numbers, reside together. A new class of hostel has been established at Calcutta by the Oxford Mission (p. 105) and at Allahabad by the C.M.S. These are not attached to any Christian college, but receive non-Christians attending non-Christian colleges. This is an important development, which the Government highly appreciate and have liberally helped.

VI

THE FIRST INDIAN CLERGY

In our fourth chapter, one feature of the meeting of Prince Edward of Wales (King Edward VII.) with the Tinnevelly Christians in 1874 was omitted, in order that it might introduce this chapter. In the front of those seven thousand representatives of the Tamil Church stood fifty-three men clothed in the long white garments of their country like the rest, but distinguished by a simple black scarf round the waist. Who were these? They were the Tamil clergy of the district. Most of them have died in the forty-two years that have since elapsed, but if the present Prince Edward met such a Tamil gathering to-day, he would find over a hundred, and if we could gather together in a great synod all the Indian clergy, they would number over 300. When and how did this happy fruit of our Missions begin to appear?

It will be remembered that the S.P.C.K., when Schwartz gave Lutheran ordination to his catechist Satyanadan, to make him a "country priest" (p. 9), welcomed the act. Much more warmly would they have welcomed an ordination by an Anglican Bishop. But for that the Church had to wait five-and-thirty years. We have seen that Bishop Middleton did not consider the admission of an Indian to English orders as within his official powers, but that his successor,

Heber, took a different view, and ordained two men of Indian race. The first, however, was a native of Ceylon, and was ordained for work in Ceylon. The second, Abdul Masih, was therefore the first Indian ordained for work in India.

Sheikh Salih—that was his original name—was a Mohammedan of good family at Delhi, who had been Keeper of the Jewels to the Sultan of Oudh. Being an ardent Moslem, he went to see Henry Martyn "baited" in controversy with the mullahs; but Martyn's words in exposition of the Ten Commandments sank into his heart, and that he might learn more he took service as a copyist under Sabat, Martyn's assistant in translating the New Testament. The entrance of God's word gave light, and after Martyn went to Persia, Sheikh Salih went to Calcutta, and was baptized on Whit Sunday, 1811, by David Brown in the Old Church, taking the name of Abdul Masih (Servant of Christ). Soon after, Daniel Corrie, going up to Agra as chaplain, took the new convert with him and employed him as an evangelist. There was then no English missionary in India definitely engaged in the evangelization of the non-Christians, but the C.M.S. had sent money to a Calcutta Committee for use as required, and from this the evangelist's stipend was drawn. Manifest blessing was vouchsafed to his work, and within sixteen months he brought to Corrie for baptism fifty Hindus and Moslems. He was ordained on St. Andrew's Day, 1825, and died on March 4, 1827. Thomason, the Calcutta chaplain, had his portrait painted, and sent it to Charles Simeon, who gave it to the C.M.S. House, where it hangs to this day. It is surely a group of facts worth remembering, that the first native of India to receive Anglican orders was (1) a convert from Islam, (2) a convert of Henry Martyn's, (3) ordained by Bishop Heber.

And, remembering how often the impossibility of either a Mohammedan or a Brahman being converted to Christ was affirmed even to recent years, it is another striking fact that the second Indian to be ordained, in North India, was a Brahman. His name was Permanund, and he had been converted at Agra under the teaching of the Baptist missionary who, as we have seen (p. 16), was sent down to Serampore under a heathen guard by order of the Governor-General. That was in the same year, 1811, in which Abdul Masih was baptized; but Permanund would not accept baptism unless his infant son could be received into the Christian Church at the same time, and this of course the Baptist could not do. He came under the notice of Mrs. Sherwood, an officer's wife and friend of Martyn, and she got him employed as a schoolmaster by H. Fisher, chaplain at Meerut, also on a C.M.S. grant. At Christmas, 1816, he was baptized by that excellent clergyman, receiving the name of Anund Masih (Joy of Christ); and he was ordained by Bishop Wilson in 1836. He frequently visited Delhi and preached boldly there in the bazaars, but no recognized Church Mission was started there as yet. One of his converts was a Brahman in a Sepoy regiment, whose baptism caused "the greatest consternation," not among his fellow-soldiers, but among the British officers, and he was dismissed from the army—solely, as the published official documents show, because he had become a Christian.

But between the ordination of Abdul Masih and that

of Anund Masih in North India, there was one in the south. In 1830, when Bishop Turner, the fourth Bishop of Calcutta, visited Tinnevelly, an excellent catechist, John Devasagayam, was ordained deacon. He was not himself a convert, but an hereditary Christian, his father having been a pupil of Schwartz. He himself had been inspecting schoolmaster at Tranquebar, the old Danish station. He was the first Indian clergyman in an independent charge, the village "circle" of Kadachapuram, and he ministered there with great acceptance for thirty years. Bishop Smith, of Victoria, Hong Kong, who visited India in 1853, drew a graphic picture of him:

"It was pleasant to accompany John Devasagayam as he sallied forth—with firm step and energy of body and mind, though sixty-seven years old—into the adjoining villages and lanes, attired in his simple white dress, with the clerical badge of thin black waist-band, trudging along bare-footed over the sandy soil. He had kind speeches for all he met; but if any signs of slovenliness or dirt met his eye, or any appearance of negligence recurred to his mind, there were lectures in store for the villagers and the catechist at their head. The old man unites in a remarkable way the simplicity of the Cross with an European firmness and determination of spirit. He appears to infuse a spiritual-mindedness and vigour of Christian principle into all around him."

He left two sons in the ministry, one of whom, the Rev. Jesudasen John, was for many years pastor of the important congregation at Palamcotta. His daughter became the wife of the Rev. W. T. Satthianadhan of Madras (see p. 50).

The Church in Tinnevelly has produced quite a number of really excellent clergymen. There was no undue haste in ordaining them. Not till 1847 were two more ordained to the diaconate, Jesudasen John (just mentioned) and Devasagayam Gnanamuttu, a convert from Hinduism. Both served forty years. In 1851-1859, fourteen more, nine being converts and five sons of Christian parents. All these seventeen were in the C.M.S. Mission. In the S.P.G. districts, where the work had been so severely handicapped (as we have seen), there were only four in the same period, the first, Arulappen David, being ordained in 1854. He had then been over thirty years working as a catechist and schoolmaster, humbly and faithfully. In various examinations he again and again stood first, and few men, it is said, knew the Bible as intimately. He had great trouble with caste difficulties, and acted on many occasions with much tact. He died after eleven years' further service as a pastor, "looking to Christ with childlike confidence, and with a lively faith in the merits of His death."

Some of these ordinations took place on occasions of much interest, and some of the men were notable. Bishop Dealtry of Madras wrote enthusiastically of "the cheering and delightful scenes" he witnessed. In 1856 the ordination was held in John Thomas's great church at Mengnanapuram (see p. 33), when 1,800 persons were present, including clergymen and catechists and students of both Missions. "The ordination service, translated into Tamil, was printed and put into the hands of all the congregation. The service lasted four hours, and included two sermons, one in English and one in Tamil." This was on a

Saturday. Next day, at the early morning service, one of the new deacons, Paul Daniel, preached on Rom. viii. 1. The veteran John Devasagayam said of him: "He has got what you call eloquence, sir. He expresses his ideas in rich, suitable words. I give a thousand thanks to the Lord. His exposition of the doctrine of the Cross and the work of the Spirit was beautiful." He was quite a notable man. He knew no English, and had not been in any theological institution, but he was a man of prayer, and of great humility. He died of cholera only four years later, caught from a poor woman he had visited in her sickness.

One later ordination, by Bishop Gell of Madras, in 1869, must be mentioned, when twenty-two Tamils (fifteen C.M.S., seven S.P.G.) received deacon's orders and ten (three C.M.S. seven S.P.G.) priests' orders. No less than sixty clergymen, English and Indian, were present, an event at that time unique in the whole Mission-field. All the thirty-two men were ordained, not as agents of a foreign society, but on the title of the native Church Councils (see p. 116). The examining chaplains were two leading Tamil clergymen, one S.P.G., and the other C.M.S.

On that occasion the sermon was preached by the Rev. Devanayagam Viravagu. He and his brother, Vedhanayagam Viravagu, were converts from the Vellalars, a relatively high caste in South India. Both became Superintendents of whole Mission districts. Another leader was W. T. Satthianadhan, who was also a convert, won while he was a schoolboy. He was for many years incumbent of Zion Church, Madras, with its influential Tamil congregation (p. 117). He was one of Bishop Gell's examining chaplains, and a Fellow of Madras University, with a seat on the Senate; and Archbishop Benson gave him the Lambeth B.D. degree. When he and his wife visited England in 1878 they won all hearts. Their son Samuel came to Cambridge, and graduated with honours in two triposes. He afterwards became Professor of Logic and Philosophy in the Government College at Madras, and he was the Indian leader of the Student Movement and other Christian agencies.

South India includes also the Telugu Missions and Travancore, and the first Indian clergy there will be referred to in future chapters.

In the Bombay Presidency, Daji Pandurang, a converted Brahman, was the first ordained, in 1850, and was connected successively with both C.M.S. and S.P.G. Another Brahman convert, Appaji Bapuji, was admitted to the ministry in 1855, and was on the C.M.S. roll forty years. There were two converted Parsis, Ruttonji Nowroji and Sorabji Kharsedji, the former being for many years head of the C.M.S. Mission at Aurangabad, and much honoured by the British civil and military community there; while the latter was the father of the brilliant brothers and sisters Sorabji, now known all over the world.

Returning to North India, among others ordained more than half a century ago, the most notable by far was Krishna Mohun Banerjea, a Kulin Brahman (the highest section), and the first Bengali admitted to the ministry. He was a student in Duff's College, and the second convert there, as already related (p. 42). He joined the English Church, was ordained by Bishop Wilson in 1839, became a Professor in Bishop's College, was for seventeen years on the S.P.G. roll, and all that time, and also after his retirement, was the most influential Indian Christian in Bengal, and perhaps in all India. His *Dialogues on Hindu Philosophy* urged on the reforming members of the Brahmo Samaj the question, "Where is saving truth to be found?" He died in 1885, universally respected. Among other S.P.G. men were three able Bengalis, Gopul Chunder Mitter, B.C. Choudhury, and H.H. Sandel. The first C.M.S. man (after the early two) illustrates the mutual services often rendered by the two Societies to one another. Daud Singh was a Sikh fakir, baptized by W. H. Perkins of the S.P.G. at Cawnpore. Naturally he sought his own people, and therefore went up to the Punjab and became a catechist in the C.M.S. Mission. In 1854 he was ordained by Bishop Wilson, and was for many years pastor of the Amritsar congregation. He was the first Sikh to be baptized, and the first to be ordained. Among other North India men were three ordained together in 1859—David Mohun, Davi Solomon, and Tulsi Paul. Mohun was pastor of Muirabad, the Christian village before mentioned (p. 28), and gave valuable aid in revising the Hindi Bible and Prayer-Book. Paul, like his Tamil namesake, was a great preacher. T. V. French wrote of him:

"He is an elderly man, of majestic appearance, with a noble beard, overflowing with intelligence and beaming with kindness and love. I translate with him Butler's *Analogy*, Hengstenberg's *Christology*, and Augustine *De Civitate Dei*. He is a wonderful preacher; the people quite hang upon him."

One other C.M.S. man must be mentioned, if only

because he was the father of the present Principal of St. Stephen's College (S.P.G.) at Delhi, Professor Rudra: the Rev. Piari Mohun Rudra, who became the able and trusted Superintendent of the whole Nadiya Mission in rural Bengal. (Some Punjab men will be mentioned hereafter.)

But there is yet one more name on no account to be missed, that of one who was in some ways the most remarkable of all the Indian clergy, the Rev. Pundit Nehemiah Nilkanth Goreh. He was brought to Christ by the Rev. W. Smith, C.M.S. missionary at Benares, was trained for a time at the C.M.S. College at Islington, was ordained in 1868, was on the S.P.G. list at Calcutta for three years, and afterwards joined the Cowley Fathers at Poona. The Principal of Islington, Mr. Childe, wrote of him as a student: "He was a man of superior intellectual power. We had few more genuine Christians in our body, but none so sorely exercised with speculative doubts." His personal influence was great. Among those whom the Church of Christ owes to it were the Parsee mentioned above, Ruttonji Nowroji, the influential Mohammedan convert, Safdar Ali, and the well-known Pundita Ramabai of Poona. He died in 1895, and his old friend Dr. Hooper, the learned C.M.S. missionary, wrote: "No divergence in our way of looking at some parts of Christian truth could for a moment estrange me from one who was led by the Spirit of Christ. Men saw Christ in him."

VII

THE FIRST WORK IN THE PUNJAB

It is a wonderful thing to stand in a certain turret in the frontier city of Peshawar, and to gaze upon the mountains which mark the farthest limits of British India, and through which run the passes into Afghanistan. But this Peshawar is itself an Afghan city, and as vehemently Mohammedan as Bagdad or Khartum. What, then, is this turret, out of which we are now surveying the city, and the broad valley around, and the background of hills? Look up! See the Cross surmounting it! Yes, this is the bell-turret of a Christian church. Look around; observe upon scores of flat roofs all the signs of domestic life, yet not a living person is in sight. And did you hear the bell toll as we came up the corkscrew steps inside? What does it all mean? It means this, that when the church was built, a promise was given to the chief citizens that when anyone was coming up the bell should announce it, so that the women on the flat roofs of the surrounding houses might disappear—a kindly concession which prevented opposition to a church being built inside the walls. For this is not the church for the British soldiers and civilians: you will find *that* in the cantonments outside the city, where they all live. This is for the Indian Christians, and its minister is a convert from Islam, the Rev. Imam Shah. When and how did all this begin?

When Queen Victoria came to the throne, the Punjab, the Land of the Five Rivers (*panj* = five; *āb* = river) was governed by Runjeet Singh, the famous Sikh chieftain. The Sikhs are the followers of Nanak, a religious reformer of Queen Elizabeth's time. When Runjeet Singh died, the Sikh chiefs, encouraged by the then recent British failure in Afghanistan, invaded our territory. Two wars ensued, with fierce battles, in one of which, Chillianwallah, our army lost 2,500 men, with guns and colours. Lord Hardinge and Lord Dalhousie, two of our greatest Governors-General, were in office during the two wars respectively. Hardinge annexed a slice of the country; Dalhousie added the rest. The completed new province was, in 1849, entrusted to the two brothers, Henry and John Lawrence, the one the most brilliant soldier England has sent to India, the other one of the strongest and wisest of civil rulers. With John Lawrence (after his brother was sent elsewhere) were associated some of the finest men who have represented Britain in India, soldiers like Herbert Edwardes, John Nicholson, Robert Napier, Edward Lake, and civilians like Robert Montgomery (father of Bishop Montgomery), Donald McLeod, Richard Temple. Within eight years was accomplished the most successful piece of work ever done by British rulers in a conquered State in that space of time. The turbulent population became quiet and loyal; the resources of the country were rapidly developed; peace and prosperity reigned undisturbed; even the dangerous Afghan Frontier was tranquillized. And when in 1857 the Sepoy Mutiny suddenly burst upon India, the Punjab and its rulers were the chief instruments in God's hand of crushing the revolt and restoring British supremacy.

But this was not all. The Punjab presents the one conspicuous instance in Indian history—perhaps in the history of the Empire—of a body of British administrators going to work definitely as Christian men, scorning to hide their faith in the true God, confessing Christ before the world, and not shrinking from energetic action (in their individual capacity) for the evangelization of the people. Did they then infringe the just principles of neutrality and toleration of the British Government? Not for a moment. Hindu, Moslem, Sikh, soon understood that they were all treated with equal justice, and that no special favour awaited any who became Christians. But they respected men who, like themselves, were not ashamed to avow their own religion and desired others to share its benefits. And God in His providence manifested to the whole world the truth of His own word to Eli, "Them that honour Me I will honour."

When Lord Hardinge annexed a small section of the Punjab after the first war, the American Presbyterians, who were nearest, crossed the river Sutlej and began their Mission. About the same time, after Sindh, the country south of the Punjab, had been conquered by Sir Charles Napier, the C.M.S. began there by opening a school at Karachi. The two movements were linked by a notable circumstance. Both were committed at first to Bengali Mission agents, and both the agents had come from Duff's College at Calcutta. This was in 1849. In that same year, a number of earnest

Christian officers in the victorious army sent a circular to all the military stations and chaplains, calling for subscriptions to start a Church Mission in the Punjab, "as a thank-offering to Almighty God for His late mercies . . . in the past signal victories and the present promised blessings of peace." One of these men, Captain Martin, was wont, like Gordon at Khartum long afterwards, to shut himself up daily for a well-understood season of prayer; and knowing that while "effort without prayer is presumption," "prayer without effort is hypocrisy," he went to the newly arrived American missionaries, who had advanced to Lahore, Newton and Forman—*par nobile fratrum*—and gave them on his own account £1,000, not for their own Mission, but for *them* to forward to the C.M.S. to help it in founding an Anglican Mission. They did forward it, adding an earnest hope that the English Church would respond. Two men were accordingly sent out in 1851, one of them, Robert Clark, a Cambridge Wrangler, who thus began a career of able and devoted service that lasted almost half a century. When they reached Lahore, a public meeting was called, not by them, but by the British leaders themselves, to form a Punjab Church Missionary Association. John Lawrence and Robert Montgomery spoke; and £3,000 was collected on the spot. The day is worth noting—February 9, 1852.

But the new Mission respected the prior occupation of Lahore by the Americans, and fixed its head-quarters at Amritsar, the most important commercial city and the centre of the Sikh religion, deriving its name from the sacred tank (*amrita saras*, tank of immortality) in the midst of which stands the celebrated

Golden Temple. The first Indian evangelist employed was the Sikh fakir before mentioned (p. 52) as baptized by the S.P.G. missionary at Cawnpore, W. H. Perkins. He was afterwards ordained, and for nearly forty years the Rev. Daud Singh was a faithful pastor of the congregation that soon began to be gathered. But you might have heard a greater preacher in the Amritsar Mission church a few years ago. You might have heard Dr. Imad-ud-din, the famous Moslem moulvie, who, having at one time been all but worshipped by pilgrims from distant parts, found Christ in Christ's own "Sermon on the Mount," and was for over thirty years a powerful witness for his Divine Lord.

But what of Peshawar? The beginning there was a year or two later. Major Martin and his regiment were ordered up there in 1853, and he at once arranged a quiet prayer-meeting, which was attended by eight officers. He and the medical officer, Dr. Farquhar (afterwards Staff-Surgeon to Lord Lawrence when Viceroy), then went to the Commissioner, Colonel Mackeson, and asked leave to establish a Mission. The reply was instant, and decisive: "Do you want us all to be killed? No missionary shall cross the Indus while I am here." It was not an unreasonable attitude from the military point of view: Peshawar was a dangerous place; it was also within easy reach of mountaineers, who took a pride in killing infidels; it required a garrison of 12,000 men; no civilian was allowed there at all without special sanction; and only a few months later Colonel Mackeson himself was actually murdered by an Afghan.

To the post of danger thus vacated Lord Dalhousie

appointed Major Herbert Edwardes, who had already done signal service in the Sikh War, writing to him, "You have a fine career before you: God speed you in it." Again Martin and Farquhar went to the Commissioner's office, and again preferred their petition. "Certainly," said Edwardes; "send for a missionary; call a meeting, and I will preside myself." Robert Clark was sent for from Amritsar, and the meeting was held on December 19, 1853. It was a small one, all the more because on that very day fell the races, the sport which Englishmen take with them wherever they go. But Edwardes delivered a speech which to this day never fails to thrill the hearts of those who read it. Here are two or three sentences:

"As Commissioner of this Frontier, it is natural that of all in this room I should be the one to view the question in its public light. . . .

"That man must have a very narrow mind who thinks that this immense India has been given to our little England for no other purpose than our aggrandizement. . . . Such might be the case if God did not guide the world's affairs. . . . But the conquests and wars of the world all happen as the world's Creator wills them; and Empires come into existence for purposes of His, however blindly intent we may be upon our own. . . .

"Our mission in India is to do for other nations what we have done for our own. To the Hindus we have to preach one God, and to the Mohammedans to preach one Mediator. . . .

"It is not the duty of the Government to proselytize India. . . . The appeal is to private consciences. Every Englishman in India, as an individual, is answerable to do what he can. . . .

"I have no fear that a Mission in Peshawar will disturb the peace. . . Above all, we may be quite sure that we are safer if we do our duty than if we neglect it, and that He who has brought us here, with His own right arm will shield and bless us, if, in simple reliance upon Him, we try to do His will."

The collection at the meeting yielded Rs. 14,000 (more than £1,400 in those days), and in a few days this sum was doubled. Private soldiers as well as officers gave handsomely. Thirty officers, military and civil, at once sent a memorial to the C.M.S. Robert Clark was instructed to remain at Peshawar; Dr. Pfander (see p. 63) came up from Agra; Major Martin retired from the army after thirty years' service, and became an honorary missionary.

Thus began the Missions on the Frontier of India. In due time Peshawar saw the Edwardes College, and the hospital, and the Zenana Mission of the C.E.Z.M.S., and the brave Afghan converts (besides others), and even Afghan clergymen. And, thirty years almost to a day after Edwardes's speech, that church which we visited at the beginning of this chapter lifted up the visible Cross within the walls of that dangerous city. It was consecrated by Bishop French on December 27, 1883, and the sermon was preached by Dr. Imad-ud-din, on the words, "If I by the finger of God cast out devils, no doubt the Kingdom of God is come unto you."*

The Punjab Mission gradually extended to many parts of the Province. Noble missionaries have taken their part, such as Gordon, Bateman, Dr. Pennell, etc. We shall see something of the Medical Missions on the Frontier and in Kashmir, and of the Divinity College,

* This was Archbishop Davidson's text when he preached the annual C.M.S. sermon at St. Bride's in 1907.

and of the work of the Zenana Society's ladies, in subsequent chapters. The harvest was not speedy, nor, for many years, abundant; but there were remarkable individual converts. Of some forty who have received holy orders, more than half were ex-Moslems. At a recent Day of Intercession for Missions, the service in Lahore Cathedral was taken by five clergymen, all Indians. When the Diocese of Lahore sent its quota of official representatives to the Pan-Anglican Congress, one of them was an Indian doctor in Government service, with Edinburgh degrees, who had been a Brahman, and was converted in his youth. In recent years there has been a great mass movement, and the progress has been rapid. The number attached to the C.M.S. Missions in 1916 was 23,000.

The Diocese of Lahore comprises the whole Punjab; also the new "Frontier Province," and Kashmir, and other native States, and Quetta, and Sindh; also the great city and important district of Delhi, where the S.P.G. has one of its largest Missions. But Delhi was not included in the Punjab until after the Mutiny, and therefore is more conveniently taken in the next chapter.

VIII

THE FIRST WORK IN THREE GREAT CITIES

We now come to a great country which is in many ways the most important part of India, and which may be called in a pre-eminent sense Hindustan. This is the upper basin of the Ganges and the Jumna, from Bengal to the Punjab. It was formerly called the North-West Provinces, being, in fact, north-west from Bengal, and the name was not changed when the Punjab, still further north-west, was annexed. Since 1902 its official name has been the United Provinces of Agra and Oudh. In this extensive territory, with a population of 47,000,000, most of the famous historic cities of India are to be found. Benares, Allahabad, Cawnpore, Lucknow, Agra, are all within its borders, and so was Delhi until the Mutiny.

We have already seen the first beginnings of missionary work in these Provinces, under the auspices of East India Company's chaplains, Martyn at Cawnpore, Corrie at Agra, Fisher at Meerut (pp. 66, 46, 47). But we will now fix our attention on three cities, Delhi, Cawnpore, Lucknow. All three have links with that interesting personality, Abdul Masih (see p. 46). From Delhi he originally came; at Lucknow he served his master the Sultan of Oudh; at Cawnpore he heard the Gospel from Martyn's lips.

Delhi was the capital of the Mogul Empire which dominated Hindustan for two centuries and a half. Under the British rule it has been subordinate in turn to Calcutta, to Agra, to Lahore, until King George's memorable visit in 1911 made it the capital of all India. It now seems destined to be one of the commanding cities of the world. Apparently the first voice lifted up for Christ at Delhi in the nineteenth century was that of an able Baptist missionary, J. T. Thompson. The first Anglican was Anund Masih, the converted Brahman and second Indian clergyman in North India (p. 47). As a catechist he was stationed at Karnal, and from thence he from time to time visited and preached in Delhi. Naturally, he appealed to the Hindus. Dr. Karl Pfander, from Agra, appealed to the Mohammedans, with whose mullahs he disputed in the Jamā Masjid (the celebrated mosque), bringing with him his famous book, *The Balance of Truth*, best known by its Hindustani name, *Mizan-al-Haqq*, which he had first written in German and Persian and then translated for the Moslems of India, afterwards also into Arabic, Turkish and English. Pfander was perhaps the greatest of missionaries to Mohammedans. Sent by the Basle Society to Persia, and turned out of that country, he went to India, joined the C.M.S., received Anglican orders from Bishop Wilson, and afterwards served at Constantinople. Such a pioneer at Delhi deserves commemoration.

Then appear three able Indian Christians there, before a regular Mission was established: Ram Chandar, mathematical teacher (afterwards Professor) in the Government College, who had been converted to Christ through noticing the reverent worship of the

English congregation; Chaman Lal, Government assistant-surgeon, a convert from Duff's College; and Wilayat Ali, a catechist in charge of the Baptist Mission in the absence of any European. And these three did what they could, supported by the chaplain, M. J. Jennings, who had baptized the two former. But in 1854 the C.M.S., unable to add to its already occupied stations, "rejoiced to announce"—the words of its next Report—that the S.P.G. had undertaken a Mission in the great city.

The S.P.G. sent two Cambridge men, Jackson and Hubbard, worthy precursors of the great Cambridge Mission by-and-by to follow. They were to found a missionary college. But on May 11, 1857, the Mutiny broke out, and Jennings and Hubbard and two lay catechists (Jackson had left), and also Chaman Lal and Wilayat Ali, were murdered, with many others of the English community. Of the horrors and struggles of that year this is not the place to speak. But two facts must not escape notice in passing. First, it was the Punjab and its bold Christian rulers that had the largest share in beseiging and capturing Delhi, at the sacrifice of John Nicholson's life. Secondly, as a reward for this great service, the Delhi district was from that time included in the Punjab.

As soon as the city was restored to its normal life, Ram Chandar, who had escaped the massacre, actually started a good High School, at which English and Persian were taught as well as Urdu and Hindi, and Christian instruction given; and when the next S.P.G. missionary Skelton, another Cambridge man, arrived, in 1859, he found all in working order, with fifty-six pupils In the following year came R. R. Winter, an

Oxford man, who for many years continued the head of a fine and growing Mission, much helped by his devoted wife, a daughter of T. Sandys, a veteran C.M.S. missionary at Calcutta, and also by the Rev. Tara Chand, who had been converted through the influence of Ram Chander. Of Mrs. Winter, Bishop French, who officiated at her funeral, said that an Apostle would have gladly testified, "I give thanks for her, and likewise all the churches of the Gentiles."

Such were the beginnings of Delhi as a Mission centre. But another beginning, much later, brought it a great accession of vigorous life. In 1878 came the Cambridge Brotherhood, the first University Mission in India (see p. 102). With the reinforcement thus provided, and with the Community of Women that followed, the S.P.G. Delhi Mission developed and expanded in all directions. Other towns in the district were occupied, notably Karnal, Rewari, Rohtak; and churches and schools were built. St. Stephen's College grew into one of the finest institutions in India, and now has an Indian, Professor Rudra, as its Principal. St. Stephen's Hospital for Women was erected in memory of Mrs. Winter, the first stone being laid by the Duchess of Connaught, and the building opened by the Countess of Dufferin. The Bickersteth Hall, in the heart of the city, is an evangelistic centre, and in it open discussions have been held with the champions of Islam on Friday afternoons, the Moslem sacred day. The present writer recalls a certain Friday in January, 1893, when that hall was crowded with Mohammedans, and Mr. Lefroy, skilful, patient, unwearied, was the one defender of the Faith. It so happened that a blind mullah who had been a leading antagonist had yielded to Christ and boldly come out on the Lord's side, and the crowd had been yelling at him. For five hours the debate went on—a scene never to be forgotten!

Let us turn to Cawnpore, a name of horror in the memory of those who can recall that terrible year 1857, and the massacres of English ladies and children; yet a name of thankful interest for all who care for the extension of Christ's Kingdom, because there Henry Martyn preached to Hindus and Mohammedans, and from those preachings came, directly or indirectly, several of the earliest Indian evangelists. Of one, Abdul Masih, we have already told the story (p. 46).

But after Martyn left, his influence remained. He had roused some of the English folk, civil and military, to a sense of their Christian responsibility, and they longed for a missionary who would learn the language and devote himself to the evangelization of the non-Christians. Many years elapsed, however, and it was not until 1833 that, at the request of Mr. White, the military chaplain, the S.P.G. sent J. J. Carshore; but he found a little work already being done by an Indian catechist, with five schools and twenty-two Christians. Under him and his successors the Mission was gradually developed. One of these, W. H. Perkins, has already been mentioned (p. 52). Mr Perkins's son became Commissioner of Amritsar, and after thirty years' Government service joined the Punjab Mission as an honorary missionary, and was ordained. In the Mutiny the Cawnpore Mission was wrecked, and among the victims were two S.P.G. missionaries, Haycock and Cockey, and the former's mother, and the chaplain, Moncrieff, with his wife and child.

Although the Mission was soon revived when the great storm had passed over, it was long undermanned, and made but slow progress, though two Indian clergymen did excellent work—Samuel Sita Ram, a Brahman convert from Lucknow, and Roger Dutt, a member of the well-known Dutt family at Calcutta. But in 1889 arrived two of the four sons whom Bishop Westcott gave to India, and under them the whole work expanded. The High School became a first grade college in connexion with Allahabad University; the industrial agencies developed into a famous model; the orphanages proved a great blessing; the work among women was much extended. The women's hospital broke down prejudice and opened many homes, and the self-sacrifice of its workers was manifested when the English woman doctor and nurse, and two Indian helpers, fell victims to the plague while ministering to the plague-stricken people. The brothers Westcott are now the Bishops of Lucknow and Chota Nagpur respectively.

Then, Lucknow. The Kingdom of Oudh had been annexed by Lord Dalhousie in 1856. Its misgovernment had been terrible, and Dalhousie declared that "the British Government would be guilty in the sight of God and man if it were any longer to aid in sustaining by its countenance an administration fraught with suffering to millions." Sir James Outram had been the Resident at the corrupt Mohammedan Court, and when he was sent to Persia in command of a British expedition, Lord Canning (who had succeeded Dalhousie) appointed Henry Lawrence (see p. 55) Chief Commissioner. Lawrence reached Lucknow on March 20, 1857, only a few weeks before the outbreak of the Mutiny; but in that brief period, with heavy responsibilities on him, one of his first acts was to invite the C.M.S. to come and start an Oudh Mission in the city.

When the Mutiny broke out, Henry Lawrence found himself beseiged in Lucknow, and the heroic defence of the Residency is one of the thrilling episodes of British history. Lawrence himself was killed, and when Havelock and Outram fought their way into the beleagured enclosure, they could not get out again till Colin Campbell relieved them. Among the engineer defenders was George Hutchinson, afterwards General, and eventually a Secretary of the C.M.S.

When Oudh was reconquered, Lord Canning appointed to the Chief Commissionership one of the great Punjab men, Robert Montgomery (see p. 55). In March, 1858, Lucknow was reoccupied; in April Montgomery entered on his office; and actually on the 20th of that same month he wrote to the C.M.S. renewing Henry Lawrence's invitation. In response, Leupolt of Benares was ordered to go up. He was just on the point of starting for England on furlough, his wife having already gone. Oudh was still full of rebels, and Colin Campbell's troops were still engaged in dispersing them; and the Benares Christians wept at the thought of their beloved Padre going into such danger. But to Leupolt such an order was simply to be obeyed, wife or no wife, furlough or no furlough, health or no health, peril or no peril. In the heat of August he drove all the way in his little open trap, David Mohun (see p. 52) accompanying him. Montgomery warmly welcomed him, and put one of the many deserted palaces at his disposal, the "Zahur

Bakhsh" (fully occupied to-day by mission quarters, schools, etc.). A public meeting was held, many officers attended, large contributions were given; the distant guns telling what the troops were still doing. When Leupolt officiated at the Sunday service, all the men present were armed, and as the communicants went up to the Holy Table, their swords or muskets were laid down till they came back.

Lucknow has been the centre of active evangelization ever since. In 1893 it gave its name to a new Anglican diocese, and two missionaries became Bishops in succession, A. Clifford of the C.M.S. and G. H. Westcott of the S.P.G. In 1911 an important Conference was held in the city on Missions to Mohammedans in all parts of the world, the Report of which is a mine of valuable information.

Several other cities in these great Provinces have interesting missionary histories: Banda, Rurki, and Moradabad, S.P.G.; Benares, Gorakhpur, Azamgarh, Faizabad, Allahabad, Agra, Muttra, Aligarh, Meerut, C.M.S. The three we have visited are specimens.

IX

THE FIRST WORK AMONG THE HILL TRIBES

If we travel by rail from Calcutta some 150 miles northward, and arrange for the train to stop at a particular spot where there is no station, we shall find ourselves among a people quite different in appearance from the Indians we have met so far; nearly black in colour, almost African-looking, with great black eyes. We see no signs of idolatry, but upright stones smeared with red paint are the outward tokens of religion, which in fact is a sort of animism, belief in and fear of evil spirits. But presently, on a hill, we see a great church, with a tower visible miles away; and if it is Sunday, and we stand at the church door, we shall see little companies of these people coming over the hills from their distant villages. In their own little chapels or prayer-huts they gather day by day, but on Sunday they walk these many miles to join joyfully in the common worship of the true God. They fill the great church, and when the time for the offertory comes, they will bring their gifts in kind—grain, rice, etc., and perhaps a live kid—up to the Holy Table.

Who are these people? and how came God's great Message to reach them? Their forefathers were in India long before the Hindus or Mohammedans. They belong to the original inhabitants, the non-Aryan

Hill Tribes. We are in the Rajmahal Hills, and these are the Santals. But they live in the valleys, or on the slopes. If we go up to the tops of the hills, we shall find a different tribe, with a different language, known as Paharis; but Pahari is really a generic name for any hill-people. They were the terror of the countryside in former days, until in 1780 Warren Hastings, the famous Governor-General, sent to them a young civil officer, Augustus Cleveland, who was successful in taming them by kindness. The Government then marked off a large area of the hill-country, to protect them from the oppressions of the Hindu landowners, and invited the Santals from a district farther south to come and occupy the valleys.

But taming is not evangelizing, though it may prove a step towards it. It was Bishop Heber who thought of their evangelization. He sent the Rev. T. Christian, one of the first two S.P.G. missionaries in North India (other than for Bishop's College) to carry the glad tidings to the Paharis; and Christian quickly won their confidence, and began a promising work; but his early death left them without a teacher for many years. Then Sir George Yule, the Commissioner of the district, having suppressed an insurrection of the Santals provoked by the exactions of Hindu money-lenders, bethought himself that the best cure for unrest is the Christian Faith. He applied to Droese, a Berlin Lutheran who had been ordained by Bishop Wilson and was in charge of the C.M.S. mission at the nearest big town, Bhagalpur on the Ganges, and asked him to come and open schools.

At last, in 1860, appeared the real founder of the Santal Mission. This was E. L. Puxley, an Oxford man who had been a cavalry officer, and had served with his dragoon regiment in the Crimean War. He offered his services to the C.M.S., and was commissioned to Lucknow, the very place for a soldier (see p. 69); but on his voyage out some officers on board awakened his interest in the Santals, and to them he presently went. He began, like Mr. Christian before, promisingly. He bought with his own money from the railway company some buildings at Taljhari; he made a first translation of St. Matthew's Gospel and parts of the Prayer-Book; he formed a class of boys to be trained as teachers, and from that class came the first two converts, who eventually became the first two men ordained in the country. But Puxley was struck by the jungle fever, and ordered back to England to save his life. He was succeeded by W. T. Storrs, who built that church on the hill above mentioned. Among other good men must be mentioned H. W. Shackell, Fellow of Pembroke, Cambridge, who, like Puxley, extended the Mission Stations at his own expense; and F. T. Cole, who lately died after forty-five years' valuable service, particularly in translational work. He was an Hon. Canon of Calcutta.

To the south-west of the Santal country is a much larger district, Chota Nagpur, inhabited by many tribes to which the Hindus gave a common name, Kol—*i.e.*, pig-eater. To them, in 1845, came four young Germans, sent from Berlin by a remarkable man, Pastor Gossner, who had been a Roman Catholic priest in the Tyrol, but had been excommunicated for his "liberalism," and whose heart was filled with longing for the evangelization of the world. From his one church in Berlin went forth Missions to West Africa, India, the Malay Archipelago, and New Guinea, sustained by the prayers and offerings of his people.

The little band settled at Ranchi, the chief town, living in the most frugal simplicity. Five years passed away, and they were still learning, praying, and tending orphans. Then four Kols said they wanted to "see Jesus," but failed to understand that He could only be seen spiritually. Then three others came, and observing that the "sahibs" worshipped without "seeing Jesus" with bodily eyes, came under instruction, and were baptized in 1850. Many followed in their steps, not all for the sake of Christ, but in hopes of improving their social condition—a motive by no means to be despised, seeing that it so often leads on to what is higher and better. In the next few years 700 joined the little Christian community; and after the Mutiny of 1857, in which they were scattered and suffered much, the numbers rapidly increased.

But Pastor Gossner was now (1857) in his eighty-fifth year, and found the direction of the Mission beyond his strength. He appealed to the C.M.S. to take over the whole work, the missionaries and the converts being quite willing to join the Anglican Church. The Society, however, could not add to its already heavy responsibilities; but it voted him £1,000 from a special India Fund raised after the Mutiny; whereupon a new committee was formed at Berlin. But after the aged saint passed away, the new men sent out belonged to the younger and rationalistic school of Lutherans, and friction ensued in the Mission. The older men approached the Bishop of Calcutta, renewing the request to be taken over by the English

Church. Bishop Cotton went to see them, and was present at the baptism of 143 candidates. The Te Deum sung by the large congregation filled him with astonishment, and he wrote: "The effect of that grand verse, 'The holy Church throughout all the world doth acknowledge Thee,' sung by these people reclaimed from savagery, was quite sublime." But for a time nothing could be done.

Eventually Bishop Milman, who succeeded Cotton, consented to receive the aggrieved section, and the S.P.G. undertook the charge of them at the Bishop's request. On April 17, 1869, he welcomed 7,000 Christians into the Church by confirming the communicants among them, gave Anglican orders to three Lutheran missionaries, and ordained a native deacon, Luther Daoud Singh. The younger Germans continued their own Mission, and friendly arrangements were made to prevent future friction. The Rev. J. C. Whitley, of the S.P.G. Delhi Mission, came to superintend the new work, and progress continued happily. In the next six years ten Kols were ordained. The German veterans eventually retired in broken health, the senior, F Batsch, after forty years' service. When he first came to the country there was not a single Kol Christian. When he left there were over 40,000. Here, too, we again see the value of the co-operation of civil and military officers. Colonel Dalton, the author of *The Ethnology of Bengal*, was the great friend of the Mission. On the other hand, the S.P.G. Reports give a painful account of the aggressions on it of the Jesuit missionaries.

In 1890-1891 two events occurred of great importance to the Mission. Bishop Johnson of Calcutta arranged for the formation of a conventional diocese within the legal boundaries of Calcutta Diocese, and Mr. Whitley was consecrated first Bishop; and Dublin University organized an University Mission to join the S.P.G. in Chota Nagpur, which has given the work a fine succession of able Hibernian missionaries, introduced the happy influence of doctors and of devoted women, and aroused the deep interest of the Church of Ireland.

The European war has wrought a great change in Chota Nagpur. The Germans of the Lutheran Mission have been necessarily deported, and the present Bishop of the Anglican Mission, Dr. Foss Westcott, has courageously undertaken the supervision of their work, educational and pastoral, refraining in a generous spirit from "proselytism," and leaving the Kol Lutheran pastors to administer the sacraments to their own people, whose numbers have largely increased in recent years. That is the true spirit of Christian brotherhood.

South-west again of Chota Nagpur, we come to the extensive hill districts comprised in the Central Province and the contiguous native States. These are partly peopled by the Gonds, another large non-Aryan nation, and their district is known as Gondwana, on which Bishop Chatterton of Nagpur, the diocese which includes it, has written a valuable book. In 1860, Colonel (afterwards Sir Arthur) Cotton, who was engaged in irrigation works on the Godavari river, applied to the C.M.S. for a missionary for the Kois, a branch of the Gond people, thus again illustrating the good influence of officers who are earnest Christians "Two things," he wrote, "are wanted to make this country a garden—the natural water and the water of life." One of his assistants, Captain (afterwards General) Haig induced some of the subordinate officials to unite with him in prayer about it, and one result was the conversion of a Hindu Rajput, who was head of the local commissariat department, and who was eventually ordained—the Rev. Vencatarama Razu. Missionaries were sent, one of whom was afterwards well known as the learned Chancellor Edmonds of Exeter. Another, John Cain, died lately after forty-seven years' service. His excellent wife from Australia is one of the recipients of the Kaisar-i-Hind medal. There are some 2,000 Christians, but the majority are not Kois, but of the Telugu race.

For the main part of the Gond people, Sir Donald McLeod, another of the benefactors of Missions, provided at his own expense, in or about 1850, a party of six German artisans with wives and families to form a Christian agricultural settlement; but all except two were carried off by cholera, and of these two, one became insane. Not till 1879 was the C.M.S. Mission established; of which, owing to famines and epidemics, the chief agencies have been the hospital, the leper asylum, the orphanage, etc; and the results in figures are small beside those of the Chota Nagpur and Santal Missions.

One more non-Aryan tribe must be introduced, the Bhīls of Rajputana. The Mission to them was started on the strength of a gift to the C.M.S. of £1,000 by E. H. Bickersteth, afterwards Bishop of Exeter. C. S. Thompson was sent out in 1880, laboured with rare self-sacrifice twenty years, and died of cholera under a tree in the jungle in 1900. He left only sixteen Christians as the fruit of his work, but his patience and gentleness had opened the way to a people who had at first taken him for a government agent sent to tax or to kill them; and others entered into his labours. One of these was Arthur Outram, grandson of Sir James, the hero of Lucknow. The leading missionary for some years, A. I. Birkett (who was drowned lately in crossing a swollen river), was successful in organizing a self-governing Bhil Church, and his wife's medical qualifications were a great blessing. A Hindu revenue-officer declared that nothing but Christianity could have so transformed such barbarians. All these hill people might well worship and praise Him who "remembered them in their low estate."

X

THE FIRST WORK AMONG WOMEN

It is a fact little realized that there are more women missionaries in the field than men. In the case of married couples, of course, the two sexes balance one another, and the single women are now more numerous than the single men. Are *now* more numerous: yes, it is a new fact. There is another fact, not a new one, but as old as the human race—viz., that half the population of the world consists of women; and this fact, familiar as it always has been, seems never to have been realized, or at least its bearing understood, in those earlier days. The common idea was that a missionary was normally an ordained man. "Lay missionaries" were unknown in the Church of England. A schoolmaster or an artisan might be sent out for some particular secular work, but he was not reckoned as a missionary, not even like the Roman "lay brothers"; and naturally women shared the disqualification. And all the while it was forgotten that in most non-Christian lands the women cannot be effectually reached by male missionaries, so how were half the population to hear the Gospel?

But were there not the wives? No doubt many of them actually did important work, but it was, so to speak, by the way. They were not counted; their primary occupation—rightly enough—was the care of husbands and children and households. At the Anglican Missionary Conference in London in 1894, one of the speakers said that he had asked a wife what was her work in the Mission, and that her reply was, "I mind my missionary." Truly many missionaries have been saved from sickness and death by being thus "minded." But meanwhile, what of half the population of the world? And, again, many missionaries are unmarried, a condition which has its own disadvantages as well as advantages.

Let us see how the great change has come about, so far at least as India is concerned.

It was in 1815 that the C.M.S. received its first offer of missionary service from women. Three ladies at Clifton offered to go anywhere in any capacity. Daniel Corrie, the East Indian chaplain (p. 17), who was at home at the time, and who showed a sense of vision in this as in other matters, urged that there was work in India waiting to be done; but the Society declined to send unmarried women abroad, except sisters accompanying their brothers. Twenty years later than this, Bishop Wilson "objected on principle to single ladies coming out, with the almost certainty of their marrying within a month." "I imagine Tryphena and Tryphosa, and the beloved Persis, remained at home." He conveniently omitted Phœbe, who certainly did not stay at home!

From early days an exception was made in the case of girls' schools. If possible, a missionary's sister or daughter was thus employed; but other women had also to be found, and we have already seen how Miss Cooke began in Calcutta in 1820, following the good example of the wife of Marshman of

Serampore. When other girls' schools were opened, Eurasian teachers were engaged for them. But any direct evangelistic work among adult women seems never to have been thought of. In 1834, the first Society, formed mainly by Churchpeople in England, for sending women into the Mission Field, was only "for the Promotion of Female Education in the East"; and the next, many years later, was called "The Indian Female Normal School and Instruction Society." However, many excellent women sent out by these two Societies, who lived to be veterans, by no means confined their efforts to school work. Through the children they reached the mothers.

Apparently the first to attempt definite missionary work among adult Indian women was a lady quite independent of any Society. This was Miss Bird, sister of R. M. Bird, Commissioner of Gorakhpur, one of the most trusted of Anglo-Indian officials—"a born leader of men," says Sir R. Temple—who helped to train John Lawrence and William Muir. She and her brother were aunt and uncle of Mrs. Isabella Bishop (*née* Bird), so famous in later days as an intrepid traveller and brilliant advocate of Missions. Miss Bird was a delicate woman, but a devoted worker from 1824 to 1834, when she died of cholera. Whether she ever succeeded, or tried, to enter a zenana—the only way of reaching the higher castes—does not appear. Leupolt of Benares (see p. 68) used to say that his wife, an Englishwoman sent out by the Female Education Society, was the first to pass within the strictly guarded curtains. Not a few of the F.E.S. ladies did marry, as Bishop Wilson foretold; but they mostly married missionaries, and this did not stop their work. So also did the daughters of veteran messengers of Christ, like Miss Sandys, whose father was a C.M.S. man at Calcutta, and who became the wife of R. R. Winter, the distinguished S.P.G. missionary at Delhi, and did noble service there (see p. 65).

In the middle of the century, the question of educating Indian women who were already married became urgent. It had been disreputable for a Hindu lady to read or write, as the only women who could do so were the nautch girls. In this matter the Parsees of Bombay and the Christians of Tinnevelly were ahead of the Brahmans and wealthy Hindu landowners. Certainly the Missions in the South had quite thrust out of date the old saying, "From the beginning of the world it was never known in Tinnevelly that a woman could read." But the high caste boys who had received a good English education on Duff's system wanted their wives to be not wholly illiterate. The Rev. Krishna Mohun Banerjea (p. 51), to whom they listened despite his Christianity, did good service in calling their attention to the importance of women's education. The Government opened a school for caste women, who were carefully conveyed to and fro in closed carriages; but this proved a failure, and it became clear that they must be taught, if at all, in their own homes. To train Eurasian teachers for this special work a Normal School was opened at Calcutta in 1852, and it was from this effort that the I.F.N.S.I.S. above referred to was developed. But it was an English teacher in this School, Miss Toogood, who, knowing Bengali well, first obtained entrance to a Calcutta zenana, being engaged for the purpose by the first Hindu to open his house, Babu P. Cumar Tagore, in

1854. A little later, Dr. Duff opened a High School for girls, like the official one that had failed, but avowedly teaching Christianity with Miss Toogood as head mistress. Many Hindus sent their daughters to it, recognizing its high moral tone, and after the first year an examination was held in the house of a Hindu millionaire, before the élite of native society.

A curious incident occurred in 1860. Three sisters from Dublin went out independently to work under Mr. and Mrs. Leupolt (p. 68) at Benares. Their coming to that great centre of Hindu idolatry caused a sensation. "They don't wish to marry," said a Hindu gentleman to Leupolt; "they don't want money, nor fame; yet they are at work night and day: what did they come for?" But one of them became seriously ill, and all three went home.

At last, in 1861, the first steps were taken, by the I.F.N.S.I.S., to send out English ladies definitely for Zenana visiting and teaching. Seven years later, when the first public meeting of the Society was held in London, with Sir Bartle Frere as chief speaker, it was reported that nine English women, twelve Eurasians, and thirteen Brahman widows were at work; and from that time progress was steady, especially after the formation of the Church of England Zenana Missionary Society in 1880. Many devoted women went out, one of whom was Miss Charlotte Tucker, the "A.L.O.E." of young people's literature, and sister of a former Commissioner of Benares. She was already past middle life, yet she laboured zealously as an honorary missionary for eighteen years, and died at her post, Batala in the Punjab, in 1893. The Bishop's chaplain, Mr. (now Archdeacon) Brook Deedes, said that she "realized Kingsley's beautiful conception of the Fairy Do-as-you-would-be-done-by among the water-babies." Another lady, Miss Bielby, seems to have been the first to engage definitely in medical work, beginning in 1876 at Lucknow, where in her first year she paid over 1,000 visits in 150 houses besides seeing other patients at her own quarters. One of the Christian Indian helpers was Miss Golak Nath, daughter of a highly respected minister of the American Presbyterian Mission, who became the wife of the Rajah of Kapurthala, Sir Harnam Singh, K.C.S.I.

Meanwhile the S.P.G., at its principal stations, was also beginning work. Mrs. Winter at Delhi, and Mrs. Caldwell in Tinnevelly, were especially effective; and in 1863 the former organized zenana visiting by Indian Christian women, and also began simple medical treatment of the Indian ladies she visited. It was soon after this that the Society at home took the matter in hand energetically, and "The Ladies' Association" was formed in 1866. The Hon. Secretary, Miss Bullock, daughter of the chief Secretary of the Society, devoted more than a quarter of a century's valuable labours to its service. It sent its first women missionaries to India in 1868. They gradually engaged in all branches of work among women. Zenana visiting was diligently carried on; High Schools for girls rivalled those for boys; and the school at Nazareth in Tinnevelly (see p. 31) was the first in South India to send pupils to the matriculation examinations of Madras University. Boarding schools for Christian girls also provided many teachers for elementary schools. Zenana hospitals were planned, and eventually proved a blessing to both bodies and souls. Village visitation was undertaken in many districts. Indian school-teachers, Bible-women, nurses, were trained. Miss Angelina Hoare's self-sacrificing toil in the swamps of the Sundarbans, south of Calcutta, should be specially remembered. The Society has also helped the Mission among Eurasian women carried on at Lahore by the St. Hilda's Community. Several other Communities and Sisterhoods are at work elsewhere (see p. 106).

All this time the C.M.S. continued to regard the sending forth of women missionaries as outside its province, relying on the existing Women's Societies already mentioned. But in 1887 it was compelled by the needs of other Mission Fields in which these auxiliary associations were not at work, particularly Africa, to consider the many offers of service from ladies well educated and experienced in home Mission service. It had then about twenty single women in the field, most of them widows or daughters of old missionaries, who had always been welcomed. In the past thirty years it has sent out nearly 1,000 women, and 450 are at work to-day. At first, while they were sent to Africa, China, Japan, and other fields, India was still left to the auxiliary associations, but the continually increasing demands from the Missions there again forced the Society's hands, and have since claimed nearly a third of the whole number. As all the C.E.Z. ladies, and several of the Z.B.M. ladies work in connection with C.M.S. Missions, the total number of single women engaged in them in India is about 300.

Meanwhile, let not the devoted work of the missionaries' wives be forgotten. Some of them find mention in other chapters. It would be invidious to pick out individual names here.

This chapter began with the remark that women are one-half of the population of the world, and that therefore they deserved a full proportion of our evangelistic efforts. But in India, at least, they enjoy, and exercise, much more than half the religious influence. It is they, in a Hindu household comprising perhaps thirty or forty people, who see that the family gods are daily worshipped, and who teach even the children in arms to worship them. It is they who see that the ever-recurring festivals are observed; that the birth, marriage, and funeral rites are duly performed; that caste is not broken. It is the influence of wife and mother that keeps multitudes of men who are convinced of the truth of Christianity from publicly acknowledging it. To win the women would be to win India.

XI

THE FIRST DIVINITY COLLEGES

WE have made the acquaintance of some of the Indian clergy, but we have not yet seen how and where they were trained. The fact is that most of the earliest ordained men were not trained at all, if by training we mean a systematic course in a regular divinity college. Such institutions belonged to a more advanced stage in the Missions.

But there was one exception—Bishop's College, planned, as we have seen, by Bishop Middleton, and to which the Societies made such handsome gifts (p. 24). It was in full work before any Indian had been admitted to the ministry of the Church. It was not, however, a theological college pure and simple. Middleton had two designs for it: (1) to train Christian students "in the doctrine and discipline of the Church in order to their becoming preachers and catechists and schoolmasters"; (2) to teach "the elements of youthful knowledge and the English language to Mussulmans and Hindus," thus anticipating Duff's great scheme (p. 41). The East India Company gave it a fine site near Calcutta, upon which fine buildings were erected, and the S.P.G. sent out a learned man, Dr. Mill, to be Principal. But from the first it disappointed sanguine hopes. Perhaps its double purpose created difficulties. Certainly there were in those days scarcely any Indian Christians who could take the divinity course arranged. Bishop Wilson, several years later, worked hard for it. "Your noble college," he wrote to the S.P.G. in 1834, "is never out of my thoughts. I am labouring with my whole soul to secure its efficiency." Later still, Dr. Kay was an admirable Principal. Yet, for one cause or another, it was never a success, and after more than half a century the buildings were sold to the Government, and the College removed to more modest quarters within the city, where it took new life under the auspices of the Oxford Mission and the principalship of Mr. Whitehead, now Bishop of Madras. The Bishops are now considering fresh plans for its usefulness, and there is doubtless still a great future before it.

So we must go back to the simpler beginnings elsewhere. In the earliest stages of a Mission the training of converts for such purposes has necessarily to be done for individuals by individuals. The missionary, let us say, has a dozen adult men converts. He constantly gives them further Christian instruction. Two or three, we will suppose, show superior intelligence or exceptional stability of character, and these he attaches to himself, takes them with him on his bazaar preachings and village itinerations, gives them fuller instruction, trains their minds, invites them to help in the preaching and teaching. Or he has as yet no adult converts, but he has induced some of the people to let him teach their boys to read, and he opens a small school. Here, again, he presently picks out three or four of those whose hearts seem touched and their minds opening, and sets them to teach the others as best they may. Thus we have the embryo catechist and the embryo school-teacher. But as the Mission develops and expands, as the converts multiply, as the area of work widens, something more systematic is found necessary. Then come the Training Class for schoolmasters and the Preparandi Class for spiritual agents, and the setting apart of one or more missionaries to conduct them. And by-and-by come the Normal Institution and the Divinity College.

Both the Church Societies worked their Missions for many years without regular institutions for training, though the S.P.G. did use Bishop's College for the few men it needed in Bengal, among them Krishna Mohun Banerjea (p. 51). In the Tamil Missions in the South, which were the most forward, what was called the Tinnevelly system was gradually developed by both the Societies. Each district missionary had several village day-schools, in which Christian and non-Christian boys were taught together. Carefully selected Christian boys were brought to the little boarding-school he had at his own station, where they were further educated under his own eye. Presently the Preparandi and Training Classes would be formed at the central station; and from these, in time, came catechists and school-teachers, and from among them the candidates for orders.

The S.P.G. started a regular seminary, comprising both sections, at Sawyerpuram (p. 32) in 1844, under Dr. Pope, afterwards Tamil lecturer at Oxford; and there a great many men were trained, some of whom went on to a higher institution opened at Madras four years later. This was called the Vepery Seminary, being first started at that place, but since 1879 it has borne the more important name of the S.P.G. Theological College. Up to 1900 no less than ninety-two of its students had been ordained. Its success was largely due to the ability and devotion of A. R. Symonds, Principal from 1848 to 1874. In later years Dr. Kennet and A. Westcott held that office, and since 1900 the Rev. G. H. Smith. The college is used for both Tamil and Telugu students, the latter having received their preliminary training in an institution at Nandyal.

The C.M.S. had started a regular college at Madras rather earlier, in 1838, under J. H. Gray, and some of the ablest of the first Indian clergy of Tinnevelly and Travancore were educated there. But after ten years, when Mr. Gray retired, the Society fell back on the simpler Tinnevelly system. For a long period E. Sargent conducted the Preparandi Institution, and trained many men, who turned out excellent pastors; while the schoolmasters were educated in a Normal School, in later years under T. Kember. In 1884 a regular Theological College was opened at Madras, for the higher training of some of the clergy. H. D. Goldsmith was Principal, and latterly E. A. L. Moore.

The two Madras institutions have kept up a friendly rivalry in regard to academical distinctions. Both have entered their men for the Oxford and Cambridge Preliminary Theological Examination, and both have done well. Alike in that examination and for the Bishop's Greek Testament prizes, they have in turn taken the first places.

In North India the S.P.G. has a Theological Class at Ranchi for the Chota Nagpur Mission, which was started when that Mission was begun by J. C. Whitley, and has in recent years been conducted by his son. At Cawnpore, the Henry Martyn Divinity School has been begun. At Delhi, St. Stephen's College has been used. The C.M.S. has divinity schools at Calcutta, Allahabad, and Lahore, also a class of simpler type for the Santal Mission, also a small divinity school at Poona.

Of one of these, which in its way was a real "Beginning," more must be said. This was the Lahore College, founded by T. V. French, who was afterwards the first Bishop of Lahore.

We have already met French as founder of St. John's College, Agra, on the principles exemplified by Duff at Calcutta. Since then he had been twice driven home by severe illness. As a distinguished Oxford man he was naturally welcome at the Universities as an advocate of Missions, but he shrank from appealing for recruits unless he were also going out himself. So when R. Clark of the Punjab (p. 57) declared that "if those who ought to go won't, then those who ought not must," he once more buckled on his armour, in 1869, and went out to start another college.

But not a college like Duff's, or St. John's, Agra. This was to be a divinity college, and French had ambitious views regarding it. The Punjab Mission had only made slow progress, but it had several individual converts of superior parts, Moslems, Hindus, and Sikhs, and he believed that they could respond to a more complete theological training than had so far been thought necessary. The Hebrew Old Testament, the Greek Septuagint and New Testament, the Greek and Latin Fathers, were to be studied; and although English, with its wealth of Christian literature, was not to be excluded, the instrument of instruction was to be the vernacular Urdu. That is to say, the students were to read, say, Ezekiel in Hebrew and Ephesians in Greek, and French and his helpers were to lecture on these books in Urdu, with occasional use of Persian, Pushtu, Punjabi, Arabic, and Sanskrit. "Christianity," said French, "should be domesticated on Indian soil. A Moslem convert, prejudiced against English, should not thereby feel disqualified from theological study."

This scheme excited great interest in our Universities at home. At Oxford John Wordsworth, and at Cambridge Westcott, collected funds in its behalf. Another Oxonian, J. W. Knott, Fellow of Brasenose, who had been a disciple and friend of Pusey, and had been for a time in charge of the church built by Pusey at his own cost at Leeds, joined French, but he died at Peshawar before the college was opened. The succession was kept up by the Principals who followed French—Hooper, Shirreff, H. G. Grey, being all Oxford men; but after them Cambridge had its turn, with E. Wigram and J. A. Wood.

The College began quite modestly, but students came from all parts of India, and even Afghans and Persians appeared. Most of them had been Mohammedans, but some Hindus or Sikhs. Some were baptized Christians from infancy, being children of converts; some were the fruit of Mission schools; some had found Christ in later life. The majority, naturally, were Anglicans, but others were not excluded. All were welcome, on one condition—they must wear Indian dress. French objected to all "Westernizing." Once a catechist came in European garb, and was allowed a week to change, but, persisting, was sent away.

French lasted out five years, and before he again left India, he rejoiced to see several of his men in definite posts of missionary service. The first two to be ordained were (1) Imam Shah, who had been a most bigoted Moslem, but had been struck by the term "Our Father" applied to God—so strange a phrase in Mohammedan ears—and then had been led to Christ by the Rev. Daud Singh (the Sikh baptized at the S.P.G. Cawnpore Mission, p. 52),—and who has since been for forty years pastor of the native congregation at Peshawar; (2) John Williams, a Christian-born Indian doctor, officially qualified, employed by Government on the Afgh n Frontier (see p. 100), but who joined the C.M.S. on a lower stipend. Among later men was J. Ali Bakhsh, who became tutor in the College, and is now Canon of Lahore.

In one thing French was mistaken, as his successor Hooper found out. Lahore could not supply all North India. For this reason: by the use of Urdu as the vernacular, French aimed at Islam, and he put Hebrew in the forefront, because of its affinity with Arabic, the language of Islam. But Hooper had been at Benares, and felt that the Hindu pundits ought to be dealt with in Hindi, with its philosophical and theological terms derived from Sanskrit; and they would appreciate Greek rather than Hebrew, because of its links with Sanskrit. It is a significant linguistic point. The practical result was that Hooper induced the C.M.S. to start another college on these latter lines at Allahabad, which has proved equally useful, with such Principals as Hackett, Johnston, Carpenter,

Waller, and now an Indian clergyman, the Rev. S. J. Edwin; and Indian tutors like Canon Nihal Singh and the Rev. J. Qalandar.

French himself illustrated throughout his career the importance of Beginnings. He was five times a pioneer. He founded the College at Agra; he started a new Mission on the Afghan Frontier; he established the Divinity College; he was the first Bishop of Lahore; he laid down his life in the attempt to penetrate the closed doors of Arabia. His remains lie under the cliffs of that hitherto almost inaccessible Mohammedan preserve.

XII

THE FIRST MEDICAL MISSIONS

ONE of the most picturesque scenes to be seen in India is a certain crowd of Indians, men and women and children, squatting in their familiar way in the veranda of a certain building at, say, nine o'clock a.m. It is a Medical Mission, and these are the out-patients. As they came in, perhaps an hour ago or more, each received a numbered ticket, and presently they will go in to the doctor in order. But first he comes out to them, opens his translated Bible, and gives them a short and breezy talk. Then, while one and another are called into his sanctum, you will see five or six Indian Christians sitting about among the crowd, talking or softly singing to them. We see the crippled men, the women weary and worn, the pale and sick children; we note the strong and yet anxious friends that have brought them; there they stand, or squat, or lie, patiently waiting their turn to see the great *hakīm*. It is a scene that any painter might delight to sketch.

Can we not understand how Christian philanthropy like this would commend the Christian Message to the people? Not to the patients only; to the friends and relatives also who bring them. And, still more, the work within the hospital, where the in-patients have just the same treatment that English patients have at home. So the Missions follow their Divine Master's example, both preaching and healing.

When and how did this medical missionary work begin? Regular hospitals and dispensaries are quite modern. In early days no one dreamed of such agencies. Yet even then there was a little occasional medical work. Very likely if the journals of the S.P.C.K. Lutherans in the eighteenth century were searched, some cases might be found. In C.M.S. history we find that the first two men sent to India, in 1814, also Lutherans, being temporarily located at Tranquebar, the Danishs tation (see p. 5), because neither the Danes nor the S.P.C.K. had anyone to send, treated an Indian medically; which led to his conversion, and to his becoming their first Indian helper. About the same time, Abdul Masih, at Agra (see p. 46), became widely known as "the Christian *hakīm* (physician), supplemented his preaching by spending half his stipend in procuring medicines, and healed hundreds of sick folk.

The first qualified doctor in a Church Mission in India was an S.P.G. missionary in Tinnevelly, the Rev. J. M. Strachan, M.D., of Edinburgh University. But this was long years after. He went out in 1861, was highly successful in treating cholera patients at Ramnad in the Madura district in 1865, and in 1870 opened a regular Medical Mission at Nazareth, the Christian village before noticed (p. 31). After he left to become Bishop of Rangoon, this work expanded under Mr. Margöschis, and several small hospitals and dispensaries were established in the district. In the C.M.S. part of Tinnevelly there was an Indian "medical pastor," the Rev. Manuel Cooksley, son of the Rev.

Perianayagam Arumanayagam, who died a few years ago after forty-two years' service.

But Medical Missions are few and small in South India, and indeed elsewhere among the purely Hindu population. It is among the Mohammedans of the North, who are so hard to reach by ordinary preaching, that they are especially valuable. They are also very effective among the Hill tribes. The S.P.G. Chota Nagpur Mission has hospitals for men and women, and in the C.M.S. Bhīl Mission Mrs. Birkett's medical work has done much to win that timid and suspicious tribe. Among the general population three Medical Missions stand out conspicuously. Two, at the great S.P.G. centres, Delhi and Cawnpore, have already been mentioned. The third, at Ranaghat in Bengal, was started in 1892 by Mr. James Monro, C.B., who had been a civil officer in that district, and who after a term of service at home as Chief Commissioner of Police in London, dedicated himself and family to missionary work in his old Indian sphere, at his own charges. It was a highly successful venture, and when he retired, he handed it all over to the C.M.S.

But of special importance have been the Medical Missions on or near the North-West Frontier. The "Beginning" of these was in the semi-independent state of Kashmir. The missionary-hearted British rulers of the Punjab in the sixties, civil and military, looked longingly at that adjoining country, notorious for both its beauty and its vices, to which Heber's lines applied more emphatically than to Ceylon:

> "Where every prospect pleases
> And only man is vile";

and wondered how a Christian Mission could get in there. Englishmen were only allowed there in the summer months, and the Mohammedans were exceptionally bigoted and bitter. In 1862 a memorial was sent to the C.M.S. by these faithful servants of the Lord, and among the signatures were that of the Lieutenant-Governor himself, Sir R. Montgomery, and those of Sir Donald McLeod, Sir Herbert Edwardes, Sir Douglas Forsyth, Generals Lake and Maclagan, Dr. Cust, etc. The memorial said nothing, however, about a Medical Mission; what they wanted was to get the Gospel Message into Kashmir somehow.

In 1864, Robert Clark, the senior C.M.S. missionary in the Punjab, went over the mountain passes into the far-famed Valley for the hot season, with his wife; and Mrs. Clark, with characteristic energy and without asking anybody's leave, quietly opened a dispensary on her own account, at Srinagar, the capital. She was not a qualified doctor, but she knew more than the native *hakīms*, and very soon a hundred patients a day were attending. One convert from Islam was given to them immediately, but on his being baptized the Governor of Srinagar himself organized a riot, attacked the house, and publicly whipped the people who came to it. The British Resident could do nothing, because the Maharajah pleaded that the Government of India had promised that English visitors would not "proselytize"; and every foreigner was turned out of Kashmir before winter.

But the energetic Christian officials who had signed the Memorial were not going to give up. They had been corresponding with the Edinburgh Medical Mission, a home Mission in the Scottish capital which has supplied well qualified doctors to various missionary societies, and which long enabled the United Free Church to stand first among societies in the number of its medical missionaries. A young doctor of distinction, W. J. Elmslie, M.D., responded to the Punjab appeal; but he was a Presbyterian, so how could he join the C.M.S.? The Punjab officials wrote to the Society, and begged that as they were themselves prepared to defray the whole cost of the Mission, an exception might be made in his case, "provided that he was prepared cordially to act upon the Society's principles." The Society agreed to make the exception for a layman and a doctor in the special circumstances of Kashmir, and Elmslie was to be a pioneer, just as Livingstone, also a Scottish layman and doctor, was to the U.M.C.A. in its earliest effort in Africa. In the following summer, when the Valley was open, Elmslie went in and opened his dispensary, May 9, 1865.

For seven summers the work went on. Visitors helped Elmslie, among them the Rev. A. Brinckman, an ex-army officer and honorary S.P.G. missionary, who had Kashmir much upon his heart. The Maharajah surrounded the dispensary with a cordon of soldiers to mark who attended, and also opened a rival hospital himself, which was all to the good, as there had never been anything of the kind before; but the people soon saw the difference between Elmslie's skill and Christian kindness and the Hindu doctor's rough treatment, and year after year they thronged the Mission. A few converts were gained, but when baptized were instantly expelled the country. But in 1872 Elmslie, after thus successfully "knocking," in Bishop Cotton's words, "at the only door through which the truth could enter," died while crossing the mountains.

Other doctors followed; the Maharajah's Government became more favourable; a fine hospital was built; the annual expulsion for the winter ceased; and now for over thirty years the work of the brothers Arthur and Ernest Neve has been known and admired all over India, as those understand who heard Lord Curzon's eulogy of them when Dr. Arthur Neve read a paper before the Royal Geographical Society.

Such was the Beginning of the Frontier Medical Missions. Kashmir is on the Frontier, though not a part of the North-Western Frontier Province. And now we see well-equipped Mission hospitals at Peshawar, at Bannu, at Dera Ismail Khan, at Quetta, and also at the great city of Amritsar itself; also women's hospitals in Kashmir, at Multan, at Batala, at Tarn Taran, besides many branch dispensaries. In estimating the medical work done, the true standard is the number of beds; and of them there are in these hospitals 1,200, which receive some 14,000 in-patients a year; while the visits of out-patients number about half a million a year. There are nearly thirty qualified British doctors, one-half of them women; and several missionary nurses, besides trained Indians. Part of this remarkable work belongs to the C.E.Z.M.S. Four of the doctors have received from the Government of India the first class gold Kaisar-i-Hind medal. One of them, the late Dr. Pennell, was a man of the highest distinction and character. He was a cousin of Lord Roberts, who wrote a preface both for a book of his on the Afghan tribes and for his biography—which latter work was written by his widow, one of the Sorabjis of Poona, and herself a qualified doctor now carrying on his work. Another, Dr. A. C. Lankester, has been commandeered by the Government to superintend measures to deal with tuberculosis all over India. One other should be named, the late Dr. Henry Martyn Clark, of the Amritsar Mission, who was an Afghan by birth, but was adopted in infancy by Mr. and Mrs. Robert Clark and brought up in Scotland. He was a brilliant student at Edinburgh, and became a missionary of extraordinary influence among the Moslems.

One smaller branch hospital should be mentioned. In 1868 the Deputy Commissioner of one of the Frontier districts put it up at Tank, a small town among the mountains, and applied to the C.M.S. for an Indian doctor with an official qualification. The Rev. John Williams, a descendant of an old Indian Roman Catholic family, who was so qualified, was sent, and laboured there more than thirty years. Such was his reputation among the wild Pathan mountaineers that when they raided the little town, they spared the hospital, in which some of them had been patients. This little Mission gained converts, one of them a Kulin Brahman with a notable history.

At those of the stations above mentioned where the Medical Mission has been the original pioneer, as in Kashmir and at Quetta, it has opened the way for other important branches of the missionary work. A signal instance is Mr. Tyndale-Biscoe's famous school at Srinagar, which has exercised such an astonishing influence upon the Kashmiri boys.

Thus, if Medical Missions are in themselves preeminently a work of mercy, they have again and again opened the door to the truth of the Gospel.

XIII

THE FIRST UNIVERSITY MISSIONS

Our Universities have from the first taken an important share in supplying our Missions with missionaries. As we have already seen, before any English clergyman had dedicated his life to the work of proclaiming the Messages of the true God to the worshippers of gods many and lords many in India, there were others who gave time and thought and labour to preparing the way. Among them were many able and devoted men from Oxford and Cambridge whose own appointed sphere was to minister to their own countrymen, officials and soldiers and merchants, as chaplains of the East India Company (see p. 17). And although the early English Church missionaries were mostly not University men, it is worth remembering that within the first half of the nineteenth century two Principals of Bishop's College were Fellows respectively of Trinity, Cambridge, and Lincoln, Oxford; that the founder of the Cottayam College in Travancore was a Fellow of St. John's, Cambridge, and the founder of St. John's College, Agra, a Fellow of University College, Oxford; and that two successive Directors of the C.M.S. Missions in South India were Fellows respectively of Corpus, Oxford, and Corpus, Cambridge; to say nothing of other graduates. And since 1850 the number has largely increased.*

We must, therefore, not suppose that the modern "University Missions" are the only missionary organizations with Oxford and Cambridge and Dublin and other University men on their staffs. In point of fact, the S.P.G. and the C.M.S. together have 150 graduates in India. But there has been great advantage in the Universities having also missionary brotherhoods distinctly their own.

Oxford and Cambridge united to form the first University Mission to the non-Christian world when they responded to Livingstone's appeal to them. But that was for Central Africa. The first enterprise of the kind for India was a Cambridge one.

The idea of such a Mission came from T. V. French (afterwards Bishop of Lahore, p. 90), and the idea was taken up and worked out by Edward Bickersteth, Fellow of Pembroke, son of a former C.M.S. Secretary. But the field of operations chosen was Delhi, at the suggestion of Sir Bartle Frere; and the Mission became affiliated to the S.P.G. Bickersteth himself went out in 1877, and in the same year French was consecrated to the new Bishopric in the sphere of which his original conception had thus materialized. One of his sons was afterwards a member of the Brotherhood. Among other members should be specially mentioned H. C. Carlyon, S. S. Allnutt, G. A. Lefroy, all three having now been in India nearly forty years; also A. C. Maitland, munificent benefactor of the Mission, and R. B.

* Before the first University Mission was started, 1877, the C.M.S. alone had sent to India seventy graduates of Oxford or Cambridge, forty-eight of whom had taken honours, and nine were Fellows of Colleges.

Westcott, one of Bishop Westcott's four sons given to India, both of whom (and others) died at their posts. When Bickersteth went to Japan as Bishop, Lefroy became Head of the Mission, and when he was appointed to the Bishopric of Lahore, Allnutt succeeded him as Head. Dr. Lefroy eventually became Bishop of Calcutta and Metropolitan of India.

The work and influence of the Brotherhood has been of immense value to the Delhi Mission. In fact, its members have taken the largest part of the burden, both in the city and in the neighbouring towns occupied. A Community of Women also, formed in connexion with the Cambridge Mission, has rendered most important service. But the general operations have already been briefly noticed (p. 65).

Three years after the Cambridge Mission, Oxford followed suit with a Mission at Calcutta. Its scheme was arranged by Dr. King (afterwards Bishop of Lincoln) and Bishop Johnson, then Metropolitan of India; and the first four missionaries, Willis, Brown, Hornby, and Argles, sailed in 1880. They presently formed themselves into the Brotherhood of the Epiphany, with Willis, who had been Vice-Principal of Cuddesdon, as Superior. For some years Dr. Whitehead, who was Principal of Bishop's College, was also Superior, and when he became Bishop of Madras, he was succeeded by Mr. (now Canon) Brown, one of the original four, who has continued to this day, and to whom the Mission is deeply indebted. Four other present members have served over twenty years. The present Bishop of Oxford, Dr. Gore, went out to Calcutta twice, in 1884 and 1890, to encourage the brethren by sharing the work for a short time.

Sir Lewis Dibdin, the present Dean of the Arches, has happily described the Oxford Mission as the modern counterpart of the Franciscan movement in the thirteenth century. "You may read the record of this Mission," he wrote a few years ago, "and fancy yourself back in the days of St. Francis." It has its *intensive* side and its *extensive* side. We see the former in its strict daily round of services, and in its rules for the religious life; also in its patient and prayerful efforts to deepen the spiritual life of the Indian Christians, particularly of the very imperfect Christians in the swamps of the Sundarbans, south of Calcutta, and in other parts of Eastern Bengal, where it has taken over portions of the under-manned S.P.G. districts. Some of these people had been Baptists or Methodists or Anglicans in turn, and then Roman Catholics, bribed by the latter to join the one true Church at last, and barely conscious of any difference between the different bodies.* A lady who worked among them for some years described her task as "turning mud images into human beings."

Then the *ex*tensive work has been chiefly among the students at the Calcutta University and some of the colleges, which only give them lectures, leaving them to lodge where and how they may, often in the worst quarters both physically and morally. The Brotherhood have also sought to influence the same class of young men at Dacca, the capital of Eastern Bengal, which is another great educational centre, and where the Government have been proposing to establish another University. The education given at

* So we learn from the *History of the Oxford Mission*, by G. Longridge (Murray, 1900). A later edition brings the story to 1910.

these official institutions is of course purely secular, and is prized chiefly with a view to getting Government clerkships or posts as teachers. The Oxford Mission, besides giving Christian lectures and encouraging personal intercourse, opened hostels where some of the students could live, and this system (see also p. 44) is just what is needed. Boarding-schools for younger boys, sons of Christian parents, have been added. These plans are substantially the same as those of other Missions, but they have been worked with singular devotion and tact.

But perhaps the most striking feature of the extensive work has been the publication of a weekly paper called the *Epiphany*. It was started in 1883 by Philip S. Smith, and afterwards carried on under the editorship of C. H. Walker. Both were specially valued missionaries, and both died at their posts, Walker after thirty years' service. The *Epiphany* has attained a circulation of 12,000, and exercises a wide and most important influence all over India. It is read by thinking men of all creeds or no creed at all, and its pages are open to any who have questions to ask or views (within obvious limits) to air, while it stands fearlessly and decisively for Christian truth, without a tinge of narrow exclusiveness, dealing patiently with the strange attitudes of the educated Hindu or Mohammedan; for instance, with the common feeling expressed by a Hindu who said, "It is of no consequence to me whether Jesus Christ was a real person or not. So long as I have the vision of the moral beauty which He sets before me, I do not care whether He lived or not!"

A great addition to the effectiveness of the Mission was made in 1900, when a group of ladies joined it as the Sisterhood of the Epiphany. Their work among women, both in the city and in the villages, their girls' schools, their dispensaries, their rescue work, their training of Indian mission-women, have all been prosecuted with unfailing devotion both in prayer and in practical service.

Lastly, the Mission has formed two Indian Communities on similar lines to its own, the Brotherhood of St. Andrew and the Sisterhood of St. Mary. The former, under the leadership of Father Chakravarti, has undertaken an independent Mission to the Garo tribe, living in a district adjoining Assam, its principle being "Indian men, Indian money, Indian management."

The remarkable influence of the Oxford Mission, limited as it is in the extent of the field it occupies and in the number of its members, is acknowledged on all hands. A brotherhood of the Franciscan type appeals to the Indian mind, and the mode of life adopted tells even more than the particular work done, important as that is. One new opening for it seems to be in Travancore, far away from its own sphere of labour, where the ancient Syrian Church has welcomed visits from Canon Brown and other members (see p. 112).

The Cambridge and the Oxford Missions noticed in this chapter were the first of the kind. Subsequently, Dublin University followed with the Brotherhood working in connexion with the S.P.G. Mission in Chota Nagpur (p. 75), and also with another band in China in connexion with the C.M.S. The Cowley Fathers of Poona, the Wantage Sisters there and at Bombay, and the Clewer Sisters in Bengal, are other examples of similarly self-sacrificing service.

XIV

THE FIRST EFFORT TO REVIVE AN ANCIENT CHURCH

LESS than five years ago, December 18-20, 1913, a memorable meeting took place at Calcutta, a Conference of specially elected delegates from the Christian Missions and Indian congregations in all parts of India, sixty in number, including four Anglican Bishops and seven other members of our communion, English and Indian. One of the members wrote of "an amazing sight," the appearance of "two venerable figures clad in strange and gorgeous robes that made them resemble Moses and Aaron of the coloured-picture Bible." Who were these venerable personages in gorgeous robes? They were the Metropolitans of the two branches of the ancient Syrian Church of Malabar, who had come some 1,500 miles from Travancore to attend the Conference. How this came about let us now see.

To find the "Beginning" of this Church we should have to go back a long way. A doubtful tradition claims the Apostle St. Thomas as its founder. Certainly it is very ancient. It had been a Nestorian Church, but in the sixteenth century, under Portuguese influence, it submitted to the Papacy. In the seventeenth century, however, the greater part reasserted its independence, obtained a Syrian Metropolitan from Antioch, and thus became Jacobite. In 1806,

Lord Wellesley, the Governor-General of India, sent Buchanan, the Calcutta chaplain (p. 17), to visit this Christian Church and report on it;* and Buchanan's *Christian Researches* excited much interest in England. The C.M.S. Report of 1812 called attention to the Syrian Church as "having maintained a regular Episcopal Succession from the earliest ages," and as "according in all important points with the faith of the primitive Church," and suggested that "a few learned, prudent, and zealous clergymen" might "revive the influence and faith of that oppressed community." The Society's "Orientalist," Samuel Lee (afterwards Professor of Arabic at Cambridge), was requested to compile a history of the Syrian Church, which was printed as an Appendix to the Report of 1817; and of the first six English clergymen sent to India by the Society, five were commissioned to promote the welfare and revival of that Church. Of these, one was Joseph Fenn, who gave up a lucrative practice as a barrister to be ordained for this work in response to what he felt to be a call from God, and whose six sons, all of them Cambridge men, rendered important service in after years both in the home Church and in the Mission Field. Another was Henry Baker, whose family have ever since had a large share in the Travancore Mission.

The C.M.S. charged the missionaries "not to pull down the ancient Church and build another, but to remove the rubbish and repair the decaying places." "The Syrians should be brought back to their own

* The Syrian Bishops gave Buchanan their codex of the ancient Syriac Scriptures. The Bible Society printed it for use in the Syrian Churches; and also a Malayalam version.

ancient and primitive worship and discipline, rather than be induced to adopt the liturgy and discipline of the English Church." They faithfully obeyed these injunctions. For twenty years they worshipped and communicated in the Syrian churches, with a ritual which in those days would have seemed strange to every Churchman in England. Their own children were baptized in those churches. They confined their exhortations to the correction of manifest evils. They urged that public worship should be conducted, not in the old ecclesiastical Syriac, but in the Malayalam vernacular "understanded of the people"; that masses for the dead, with the extortionate fees paid for them, should be abolished; that, with a view to a higher standard of morality, which proved to be deplorably low, the priests should be allowed to marry, as had formerly been the case, and as in the mother Church in Syria;* and that the duty of evangelizing the surrounding heathen population should be recognized—a duty neglected all through the centuries, just as it has been by other Oriental Churches in Moslem lands.

At first the reception of the missionaries was such as to inspire sanguine hopes of a real revival. In 1821 the Metran (Metropolitan) wrote to Lord Gambier, the President of the C.M.S., a remarkable letter of warm gratitude. He referred to "Mar Buchanan, the illustrious priest," and to "Priest Joseph" and "Priest Henry" (Fenn and Baker). He likened Colonels Macaulay and Monro, successive Residents at the Travancore Court, who had befriended the

* The marriage of priests had been given up under Roman influence.

Church and welcomed the Mission, to Moses and Joshua, and stigmatized the Pope as Pharaoh. The work was also heartily commended by Bishop Middleton of Calcutta, and by Dr. Mill, the S.P.G. Principal of Bishop's College, both of whom inspected it. But in 1825 the good Metran died. His successor proved hostile to all reform, and at last, in 1835, he convened a Synod, and persuaded the Church to reject formally all the counsels that had been offered, taking an oath of the members to cease all connexion with the Mission.

Then the missionaries acted like St Paul at Pisidian Antioch: "lo, they turned to the heathen." They had already sought incidentally to give the large Hindu population the Christian message, but now they were free to turn their whole attention to this evangelistic work. Among other efforts, in the place of a college which had been planned by Colonel Monro for the Syrians, and in which they had been working, they established a new one; and the Society sent out a Fellow of St. John's, Cambridge, John Chapman, to take charge of it.

Meanwhile, an earnest reform movement sprang up in the Syrian Church itself, showing that the influence of the Mission had not been wholly in vain, and many of the younger Syrians, who had been educated in the first college, were reading the vernacular Malayalam Bible. But this was not popular. One priest avowed his determination to expound the Gospel to his people in their own tongue instead of in what was a dead language to them; but when he began, the whole congregation rose and walked out. The simplest reform seemed hopeless, and some of the more enlightened, weary of this ultra-conservatism, and of the prevailing superstition and immorality, sought admission to the Anglican congregations that were beginning to be formed by conversions from the heathen. The counsel generally given to them was "Keep to your own Church, and seek its reform." Some did bravely hold on, and in later years their influence helped to promote the strong reform movement to be seen to-day. But others, some of whom had been excommunicated, could not be refused by the Mission, and in 1844, one of these received Anglican orders from the Bishop of Madras—George Matthan, an able man, who translated Butler's *Analogy* into Malayalam, and did excellent missionary service for more than a quarter of a century. He was followed by Jacob Chandy in 1847, and by four others in 1856. One of them, Koshi Koshi, translated the *Pilgrim's Progress*, and another, Oomen Mamen, was converted to Christ through reading the immortal allegory in that translation. Both these two men, long after, were appointed Archdeacons, and Archbishop Benson conferred on Koshi Koshi the Lambeth D.D. degree.

Year by year the missionary work among the Hindu population went forward, until in 1915 the number of Christians connected with the C.M.S. exceeded 53,000, with thirty-four Indian clergy. In 1879 it was felt that an Anglican Bishop was required, and an experienced missionary, J. M. Speechly, was consecrated. He has had two successors, E. N. Hodges and C. H. Gill.

In later years the Syrian Church has become divided into two sections, the old Jacobite and the new Reformed, each with its own Metropolitan. Indeed, there is also a small "Chaldean" section, and there are the few Syrians in the Anglican Church. We do well to regret all these divisions, but we shall do better to regret the real cause of them, the ultra-conservatism of an old Church that refuses the most urgently needed reforms. The whole Syrian community, numbering 700,000 souls (including those in the Roman communion), has been troubled in recent years by many free-lance missionaries from England and America, even by agents of the deluded followers of the late "Pastor Russell." On the other hand, the much lamented Rev. T. Walker, of Tinnevelly, held many "special Missions" at the request of both Metropolitans, which brought much spiritual blessing and kept very many unstable souls from being tossed about with every wind of doctrine.

Meanwhile, the two Metropolitans, realizing the need for unity, approached Dr. J. R. Mott when he visited India in 1912-1913, asking for his counsel and influence—a wonderful thing in itself; and, still more wonderful, as he had no time to visit Travancore, they and a party of representatives of all the sections actually took the long journey to Calcutta, and not only attended the General Conference as before mentioned, but also held a conference of their own under his chairmanship, which resulted in most promising plans for future harmony and united work, particularly in efforts to win the heathen to Christ. Then, in January, 1916, Bishop Pakenham Walsh, of Assam, and Mr. Sherwood Eddy, the American evangelist, held conventions by request in Travancore, with manifest blessing. The Oxford Mission at Calcutta also (p. 106) has found a special welcome from the old Jacobite

Church, and will probably, and quite naturally, exercise considerable influence over it. Altogether, it may well be that the ancient Church, divided as it is at present, has yet an important part to play in the building up of Indian Christendom.

XV

THE FIRST STEPS TOWARDS AN INDIAN CHURCH

LET us again go to Calcutta in December, 1912. There were other functions there in that month, besides the two noticed in the preceding chapter; among them these two: on December 29 the first Indian Bishop was consecrated; on the next three days there was a Conference of Anglican Bishops, with forty "assessors," clerical and lay, English and Indian. These assessors unanimously recommended that the Anglican Church in India should be named "the Church of India in communion with the Church of England," and the Bishops, accepting this proposal, resolved that "it is desirable to take steps at once for the introduction throughout the [ecclesiastical] Province of full synodical government, alike provincial and diocesan, on the basis of consensual compact." Subsequently it turned out that any action to form what might be regarded as an independent Church would be a breach of the law, the original dioceses of Calcutta and Madras and Bombay having been established by Act of Parliament; and the Bishops were reluctantly forced to the conclusion that such a scheme was "at present impossible."

Now let us see what two experienced missionaries say on this subject. First, Canon Heywood of Bombay, some months earlier:

"Are we going to organize the Church of England in India? I speak as one who loves the Church of England with all my heart. . . . But I am sure that it is not the Church of England that we are to organize in India. . . . What, then, do we need? We need a Church in India adapted to the land and adaptable to the peoples who sojourn here; a Church which holds fast to the fundamentals as laid down in the Lambeth Conference, a Church which draws largely from the rich treasury of our Prayer-Book, but provides for the needs and aspirations of the peoples here; a Church which has the wisdom, claimed by the Church of England in the Preface of our Prayer-Book, to keep the mean between too much stiffness in refusing and too much easiness in admitting any variation from it."

And then Canon Wigram of Lahore, when the scheme had been adopted, and before it was for the time laid aside:

"The convert finds it hard to get up any enthusiasm about the corporate aspect of his Christianity, so long as he has to be told he is a member of the Church of England, to him a foreign organization. . . . How much more will the non-Christian feel that Christianity represents something altogether outside his patriotic aspirations . . . ! But with an autonomous Church of India, in communion, indeed, with the Mother Church, but making its own Canons, and electing ultimately its own Bishops, the case will be wholly changed."

We must hope that in God's good providence this view of the matter will eventually prevail, and the difficulties be overcome. Meanwhile, let us briefly trace the previous preparatory steps taken in hop of the true consummation being attained.

Up to the middle of the nineteenth century the question did not arise. The Christian communities in India were small; the missionaries were the pastors, and the few Indians ordained were practically their curates. The Indian clergy and teachers, the churches, the schools, were all maintained by the Missions. But this could not go on for ever, and even if it could, it would be disastrous. If the Church in India was ever to be a power in the land, it must have at least some measure of independence, and the phrase came gradually into use that it should be "self-supporting, self-governing, self-extending." Hence the native Church Councils of different kinds that were formed. They had their imperfections, but they have undoubtedly exercised important influence. They have learned to manage the local affairs of the congregations, and to defray the pastoral expenses; while the Missions have continued to support the greater part of the educational agencies, and of the purely evangelistic work. Most of the Indian clergy, and a large number of the teachers and catechists, are now supported by the free contributions of the people, and the Bishops allow the Councils to give titles for orders.

The partial independence thus attained, it should be noticed, is independence of the Missionary Society. This is right, for various reasons: (1) It is the main business of a missionary society to spend its resources in the evangelization of the heathen of India, not in paying for the worship and pastoral care of Indian congregations. We appeal to our poor and to our children for contributions mainly for the former. (2) It is not good for the Indian Christians to have everything provided for them. In their heathen state they had to pay for their religious privileges, such as they were, and they should do the same now. (3) The pastors and teachers ought to be the employees of their own Church, and not of a foreign Society. (4) It is not only a financial matter. Indian Christians should not look to a foreign society to manage their local Church affairs. They should do this for themselves. All this does not mean that a wealthy Church should not help a poor Church. Certainly it may; certainly it should. But only so far and so long as such help is really needed.

Let us look at one Indian congregation. It has a Tamil incumbent, a convenient church, a mission-hall, schools for boys and girls; not taking a single rupee from a missionary society; administering its own affairs through a local Church Council, in which it combines with three or four other smaller congregations; the whole body served by, and supporting, four Tamil clergymen, and seventy male and female teachers; and not by any means wrapped up selfishly in local interests, but having a band of volunteer lay members, including University graduates, Government clerks, etc., who go out regularly on preaching expeditions, and through whom, year by year, the numbers are increased by new converts. This is Zion Church, Madras. The senior pastor, who is chairman of the Church Council, is a Tamil, the Rev. W. Devapiriam Clarke, B.A., who succeeded his father-in-law, the much respected Rev. W. T. Satthianadhan, and has been in charge twenty years. Not every Indian congregation, of course, is like this one, but very many others are doing well in various degrees.

Now notice an important point. These congregations, though independent of the missionary societies, are not independent of the Church of England. They are, for the time, an integral part of it. An English Bishop ordains their clergy, and confirms their baptized members. Is that enough? It is not. The ideal will not be reached until, as above indicated, there is a Church of India independent like the Irish and Scottish Episcopal and American Churches, but, like them, distinctly members of the Anglican Communion; governed by its own Bishops and Synods, with the liberty to frame its own regulations for worship and discipline.

But a perplexing question at once arises: What of the large British community in India? Are they to be outside the Indian Church? Surely not. The Church of Christ is to unite different races, not to separate them. This does not arise, or scarcely arises, in other Mission Fields. In China and Japan, and in parts of Africa, the Church is already organized, partially at least, though not wholly, independent. But in India the presence of the governing race introduces difficult problems, and these are all the graver owing to the fact that the English Church in India is so closely linked with the State that any attempt to establish an independent Church would require in the first instance an Act of Parliament to open the door for it.

Meanwhile, the Bishops are doing what they can. Although full synodical organization seems at present out of the question, Diocesan Councils are being formed, in which both the English and the Indian sections of the Church will be represented, and which will have great moral influence, though without coercive authority. And one hopeful step has been taken by the consecration of the first Indian Bishop. The new Diocese of Dornakal is in the territory of the native State of Haidarabad, and therefore not within the legal boundaries of any English diocese, so it was possible to appoint an independent Bishop to it. But the new Bishop, V. J. Azariah, is also an Assistant Bishop under the Bishop of Madras, which is in fact his official status. He is the son of a former Tamil clergyman in Tinnevelly, and he had done excellent work as founder and secretary of the Tinnevelly Church's own missionary society, and also in connexion with the Y.M.C.A. at Madras. He was consecrated at Calcutta on December 29, 1912, that memorable time already referred to, eleven Bishops laying their hands upon him. The result has so far been in every way most happy.

There is one other question. We must never forget that the Anglican Communion in India is but one of many Christian communions, and that its Indian members are but a small minority, say one-tenth of the whole, reckoning the Syrians, the Roman Catholics, and all the Protestant denominations. Must we take it for granted that all our home divisions are to be perpetuated in India? That would be a grievous issue of our Missions, yet none of us can see at present how to prevent it. Two things, however, we can do. (1) We can openly acknowledge, what many do not acknowledge, that the ideal would be one great Indian Church. (2) We can energetically, and generously, aim at as much union and co-operation as is consistent with fundamental principles. That was the object of the gatherings held in December, 1912, under the chairmanship of Dr. Mott. Every Church and denomination was free to be represented, and almost all actually were represented. And the result was the election of a National Missionary Council for mutual conference and united prayer, which has met each year since. This will at least tend to prevent friction and promote friendly co-operation. And we must continue in prayer that all may approach nearer to the fulfilment of our Lord's own aspiration, "that they may all be one, . . . that the world may believe that Thou didst send Me."

INDEX